STARTING OUT

STARTING OUT

A STUDY GUIDE FOR NEW BELIEVERS

MICHAEL DUNCAN
FOREWORD BY DR. GARY MARTIN

ISBN 13: 978-1482694321
ISBN 10: 1482694328

CONTENTS

ACKNOWLEDGMENTS

NO PROJECT IS undertaken in a vacuum. The wealth of people who have influenced and guided my steps in Christ are far too numerous to name, but there are several who stand out like a city on a hill.

First, I want to thank my wife, Patty, and our children for putting up with the time it took me to do this work. They are my inspiration and my joy.

I want to thank the churches I have been privileged to serve as either an associate or a senior pastor. Even as I have endeavored to preach the Word of God to the church, I have also learned and grown from the love and grace given to me from those whom I served.

I want to thank the pastors I have known and worked with—men who have had a great influence in my life and are worthy of respect. There are some pastors in particular who have had a lasting impact in my life and ministry: Rev. Fred Seidler, Rev. David Young, Rev. Danny Dickson and Rev. Eldon Iverson. Through these men, I have learned faith and the power of God's Word. These men epitomize the scripture that states, "Iron sharpens iron, and one man sharpens another" (Proverbs 27:17).

I must give special acknowledgment to Dr. Gary Martin, my first pastor. Gary was the man who baptized me in the Lord, discipled me in Christ and mentored me in ministry. His passion for the pure Word of God still resonates within my heart.

For all who will pick up this workbook in the quest for Christ, thank you. It is for you that I wrote this book, and it is for you that I continually pray.

Finally, to the Lord Jesus Christ, I offer my continual sacrifice of praise. It is my prayer that this work will bring God the Father and our Lord Jesus Christ continual glory.

By His grace,
Rev. Michael Duncan

FOREWORD

AN ANCIENT CHINESE proverb states, "A journey of a thousand miles begins with a single step." Michael Duncan has written a tool that will help new believers take that first step in a journey of spiritual growth and development. I believe the title to this work is no accident: *Starting Out: A Study Guide for New Believers*. Every individual who has ever answered the call of Jesus Christ to holy living had to start somewhere on the road to spiritual maturity. Some started out with an older, more mature person in the faith who taught them the fundamentals of the Christian life. Others started out in a specialized Bible study group for new believers in a church or home Bible study group. Still others started out reading everything they could on the spiritual life. The point is, we all started out somewhere.

I have known Michael for a number of years, and I appreciate his heart for discipling new believers in Christ. He is not a pastor who believes in "dipping and dropping" people who make decisions for Jesus. He wants them to grow in the Lord. He believes the best way to accomplish this is to get into the Word of God, study it, learn the basics of the faith, apply it and build on those basics every day. To that end, he has produced a *workbook*, not a *textbook*, on spiritual growth.

In this study, the new believer will be encouraged to study the Bible, engage in discipleship with a more mature believer or with a group of believers, and become an active participant in a local church. This will produce a balance in spiritual growth and support. This study also covers the principle doctrines of the Christian faith, from the basics regarding the Bible, salvation *and* assurance, prayer, worship, the church, stewardship and even the second coming of Christ! It is a well-rounded study that will help the disciple to start out right in the faith. At the same time, it will whet the spiritual appetite for a more advanced study when the eight weeks have concluded.

I commend *Starting Out: A Study Guide for New Believers* to the churches that desire a simple, clear, basic workbook on discipling new believers in Jesus Christ. I also commend the workbook to those new Christians who are looking for a starting point in their journey to spiritual growth and development.

—**Gary D. Martin**, D.Min.
First Baptist Church, Winton CA

WELCOME

═══════════════

Like newborn infants, long for the pure spiritual milk, that by it you may grow up into salvation— if indeed you have tasted that the Lord is good.

—1 Peter 2:2-3

WELCOME TO THE beginning of a wonderful journey! You have chosen to embark on a quest for a greater relationship with the Lord Jesus Christ, and for that, God will richly reward you. It is the goal of this new believer's class to provide you, the learner, with the tools necessary to help you grow up in your salvation. *Starting Out* has been developed to provide you with the opportunity to advance in your Christian growth through a weekly discipleship process, to give you resources and support in that growth, and to encourage you as you seek to gain a greater relationship with Jesus.

Each section begins with a Bible verse for weekly memorization and is divided into six daily exercises to help you develop a habit of personal Bible study and prayer. In addition, the entire study is formatted using the *English Standard Version* (ESV) of the holy Scriptures. If you are more familiar with other versions of God's Word, you may want to have both your favorite version as well as the ESV with you as you study.

For those who are participating in a group study, you will begin with a covenant agreement to be faithful to the Lord through class attendance, participation and completion of all assignments. Jesus teaches us to "count the cost" before we venture into a commitment that we are unwilling or unable to keep. If you are working through this book independently, you are also encouraged to sign the covenant agreement.

As you begin this grand adventure to discover a deep and abiding relationship with Jesus, it is my prayer *"that the God of our Lord Jesus Christ, the Father of glory, may give you the Spirit of wisdom and of revelation in the knowledge of him"* (Ephesians 1:17). The grace of our Lord Jesus be with you.

Your servant,
Rev. Michael Duncan

CHAPTER 1

INTRODUCTION

TODAY IS DAY one of *Starting Out*. As this course begins, you are encouraged to sign a covenant agreement stating that you will participate in all the required studies and tasks set forth. (You will find the covenant agreement at the end of this introductory section.) If you are in a group setting, both you and your class facilitator should sign it, agreeing to hold each other up in prayer and accountability for the duration of the course.

A. Goals of the Course

There are five goals for this course. They are as follows:

1. To build a foundation of biblical learning that will last a lifetime.

> *"If you abide in my word, you are truly my disciples, and you will know the truth, and the truth will set you free."*
>
> (John 8:31-32)

According to the passage above, what is the requirement for demonstrating that you belong to Jesus?

_____

_____

_____

What do you think it means to "abide" in Jesus' word?

_____

_____

_____

What happens if you know the truth?

_____

_____

_____

2. **To develop godly habits through daily devotions.**

> *"Practice these things, immerse yourself in them, so that all may see your progress. Keep a close watch on yourself and on the teaching. Persist in this, for by so doing you will save both yourself and your hearers."*
>
> (1 Timothy 4:15-16)

What should a Christian's attitude be concerning the development of godly habits?

_____

_____

_____

Who should know that you are pursuing spiritual growth?

_____

_____

_____

What is the result of living a godly and biblical life?

_____

_____

_____

3. To instill a system of personal accountability for each member.

> *"Let the word of Christ dwell in your richly, teaching and admonishing one another in all wisdom, singing psalms and hymns and spiritual songs, with thankfulness in your hearts to God."*
>
> (Colossians 3:16)

What is the prerequisite to teaching and admonishing one another?

_____

_____

_____

What is the distinction between "teaching" and "admonishing"? How should they both be implemented?

_____

_____

_____

What is the attitude of healthy Christian accountability?

_____

_____

_____

4. To promote healthy Christian relationships in the Church.

> *"Having purified your souls by your obedience to the truth for a sincere brotherly love, love one another earnestly from a pure heart."*
>
> (1 Peter 1:22)

How is sincere love for your brothers developed in the church?

_____

_____

_____

How does one obtain purity of life?

_____

_____

_____

How should Christians love one another?

_____

_____

_____

5. **To inspire every person to a greater relationship with Jesus.**

> *"So that Christ may dwell in your hearts through faith--that you, being rooted and grounded in love, may have strength to comprehend with all the saints what is the breadth and length and height and depth, and to know the love of Christ that surpasses knowledge."*
>
> (Ephesians 3:17-19)

Who is able to know the fullness of the love of God in Christ?

_____

_____

_____

What does it take for a Christian to know this love?

_____

_____

_____

What is the result of knowing the fullness of the love of Christ?

_____

_____

_____

B. Making the Commitment to Follow Through in Christ

> *"But I say to you, Do not take an oath at all... Let what you say be simply 'Yes' or 'No';*
> *anything more than this comes from evil."*
>
> (Matthew 5:34-37)

One of the qualities that the Lord is looking for is a dedicated honesty to fulfill our commitments. This commitment is not a vow but a covenant promise to do what we say we are going to do. Below is a covenant for both the student and the facilitator to complete before beginning this study.

Student Covenant

I promise to be faithful to the Lord through:

1. Actively working through each day's lesson.
2. Participating in the discussion and interaction of the class (if in a group setting).
3. Completing all work assignments.
4. Following the facilitator's instructions for the class (if in a group setting).
5. Prayerfully applying the principles I've learned to my daily life.

Student Signature _____ Date _____

Facilitator Covenant

I promise to be faithful to the Lord through:

1. Praying daily for each class member.
2. Preparing diligently for each weekly class meeting.
3. Providing resources for students' learning.
4. Encouraging each student.
5. Setting the example for the students in my daily life.

Facilitator Signature _____ Date _____

"Until we all attain to the unity of the faith and of the knowledge of the Son of God, to mature manhood, to the measure of the stature of the fullness of Christ.... from whom the whole body, joined and held together by every joint with which it is equipped."

(Ephesians 4:13,16)

CHAPTER 2

GETTING TO KNOW THE BIBLE

> **Memory Verse:** *"All Scripture is breathed out by God and profitable for teaching, for reproof, for correction, and for training in righteousness."*
>
> (2 Timothy 3:16)

THE BIBLE IS the Word of God. It was written to teach us about the redemptive work of God that was finished in the death, burial and resurrection of Jesus and will culminate in the return of Christ and the final and complete judgment of all creation. God, in writing the Bible, used men to pen the words, as it says in 2 Peter 1:21: "For no prophecy was ever produced by the will of man, but men spoke from God as they were carried along by the Holy Spirit." The Holy Scriptures were written by approximately 40 different men who lived in different countries at various times (1400 B.C.–A.D. 90) and who wrote in three different languages: Hebrew, Aramaic and Greek.

Through the ages, God moved the writers to center on a singular theme: His mighty work in the redemption of mankind, with Jesus as the pinnacle of that work.

DAY ONE: HOW THE BIBLE IS PUT TOGETHER—PART ONE, THE OLD TESTAMENT

The Bible, in its entirety, is a complete and compelling narration of the activity of God in the lives of people. The Bible is divided into two major components called the Old Testament and New Testament. The Old Testament is a record of God's dealing with mankind before the time of Jesus Christ, while the New Testament is God's dealing with mankind during and after the coming of Jesus.

The Old Testament is a collection of 39 books written by approximately 30 different authors. The books of the Old Testament were written to chronicle the activities of God with His creation and, more specifically, with His chosen people, Israel. The writings of the Old Testament cover about 1,000 years, ranging from 1400–400 B.C. The Old Testament looks forward to the coming of God's Messiah: Jesus.

7

A. The Pentateuch (5 Books)

The first five books of the Old Testament, often referred to as the "Pentateuch," were written by Moses around 1400 B.C. Below, list the first five books in order:

1. _____   The creation of man, entrance of sin into the world, establishment of God's nation, and promise of redemption.

2. _____   God redeems His nation, Israel, from Egypt.

3. _____   Priestly laws governing sacrifice, worship and the purification from sin.

4. _____   The wandering of God's people in the wilderness.

5. _____   Moses' final discourse as he prepares God's people to enter the Promised Land.

B. History (12 Books)

The next 12 books describe God's activity with His chosen people from the time of their entrance into the Promised Land until their captivity in Babylon. These books were written from about 1400–450 B.C. List these 12 books in order:

1. _____ 4. _____ 7. _____ 10. _____

2. _____ 5. _____ 8. _____ 11. _____

3. _____ 6. _____ 9. _____ 12. _____

C. Poetry (5 Books)

The next five books are poetic in nature, describing God's greatness and His activity among mankind. List these books in order:

1. _____

2. _____

3. _____

4. _____

5. _____

D. Major Prophets (5 Books)

The next five books are called "Major Prophets" primarily due to their length. They were written from about 750–550 B.C. List these books in order:

1. _____   4. _____

2. _____   5. _____

3. _____

E. Minor Prophets (12 Books)

The last 12 books of the Old Testament are called "Minor Prophets" due to their length, as they are shorter than the "Major Prophets." These were written from about 840–400 B.C. List these books in order:

1. _____   7. _____

2. _____   8. _____

3. _____   9. _____

4. _____   10. _____

5. _____   11. _____

6. _____   12. _____

DAY TWO: HOW THE BIBLE IS PUT TOGETHER—PART TWO, THE NEW TESTAMENT

The New Testament, or New Covenant, is a collection of 27 books written by about nine different authors. The books of the New Testament reveal Jesus Christ as God's coming Messiah, the Redeemer of mankind. The New Testament spans a period beginning with the birth of John the Baptist and culminating in the final return of Jesus and the establishment of His eternal kingdom.

A. Life of Christ (4 Books)

The first four books of the New Testament were written to chronicle the life and ministry of Jesus while He was on earth. Each book was written to convey the life of Christ to a specific group or for a specific purpose. List these books in order:

1. _____ Written to reveal Jesus as the long-awaited Messiah.

2. _____ Written to reveal Jesus as the obedient Servant.

3. _____ Written to reveal Jesus as the perfect man.

4. _____ Written to reveal Jesus as the Son of God.

B. History (1 Book)

This book chronicles the birth of the Christian church and the spread of Christianity across the world. It covers a time period from the ascension of Jesus to the captivity and imprisonment of the apostle Paul in Rome. This book was written as a companion to the gospel of Luke and is by the same author.

1. _____

C. Letters to Churches (9 Books)

These letters were written by the apostle Paul to various churches to instruct believers in the nature and practice of the Christian faith. List these letters in order:

1. _____   6. _____

2. _____   7. _____

3. _____   8. _____

4. _____   9. _____

5. _____

D. Letters to Pastors and Leaders (4 Books)

These four letters were written to individuals rather than churches. They contain instruction and requirements for leadership in the church and encouragement for those who are leading. Each of the letters bears the name of the one to whom it was sent. List these letters in order:

1. _____   3. _____

2. _____   4. _____

E. General Letters (8 Books)

These letters were written either to individuals or groups to encourage and instruct them in the various aspects of the Christian faith. List these letters in order:

1. _____   5. _____

2. _____   6. _____

3. _____   7. _____

4. _____   8. _____

F. Prophecy (1 Book)

This final book of the New Testament tells of future events. It culminates in the establishment of God's final kingdom with Christ Jesus as King, the final judgment of the wicked, and the perfection of believers.

1. _____

DAY THREE: WHY SHOULD WE STUDY THE BIBLE?

As a new believer in Jesus, it is imperative for you to grow in knowledge and understanding of the person of Christ and the nature of Christian living. God, in His infinite mercy, has given us His Word in written form so that we can adhere to His requirements and be able to know and do His will. God's Word gives us a better understanding as to the importance of studying the Bible. The term "disciple" means "learner," and that is what you are to be in your walk with Christ: a continual learner.

A. The Importance of Studying God's Word

Below are some questions to help you gain a better understanding as to why it is important to study the Bible.

Studying the Bible Will Help Us Grow

Read 1 Peter 2:2. This passage denotes a craving for "pure spiritual milk." That phrase can also read "pure milk of the word." Truly, there is no other spiritual milk than that of the Word of God.

What attitude should a Christian have toward the Word of God?

_____

_____

_____

What will the Word of God do for those who participate in it?

_____

_____

_____

Studying the Bible Will Change Us

Read John 17:17. This passage uses a term you may not be familiar with: "sanctify." Simply put, to sanctify something means to set it apart for noble or holy use. For example, in some houses there are dishes referred to as "the good china" that are stored away. The good china is reserved for special occasions and quality guests. You would never let a three year old eat from the good china, or else it wouldn't be good anymore. That is sanctification—those dishes are set apart for noble use.

How are Christians sanctified?

_____

_____

_____

How has your life changed since you began your walk with Jesus?

_____

_____

_____

Studying the Bible Will Deliver Us

Read Matthew 7:24-27. In this passage, Jesus equates living in His Word to that of security in the midst of a storm. Truly, there are turbulent times in our lives when we need to have a secure place to stand and a foundation upon which we can build our lives. Jesus describes two scenarios:

Scenario One: The Wise Builder (verses 24-25)

What two things did the wise man do with the Word (verse 24)?

1. _____

2. _____

What were the three circumstances that came about (verse 25)?

1. _____

2. _____

3. _____

What was the result?

_____

_____

_____

Scenario Two: The Foolish Builder (verses 26-27)

What two things did the foolish man do with the Word (verse 26)?

1. _____

2. _____

What were the three circumstances that came about (verse 27)?

1. _____

2. _____

3. _____

What was the result?

_____

_____

_____

What is the primary difference between the wise man and the foolish man?

_____

_____

_____

B. Six Definitive Realities of the Word of God

Read Psalm 19:7-9. In this passage of Scripture, we find a wonderful picture of the Word of God. There are six descriptions of God's Word, six qualities and six effects that are found in this text. List these in the table below.

	Descriptions	Qualities	Effects
1.			
2.			
3.			
4.			
5.			
6.			

For a more lengthy and detailed description of the Word of God, see Psalm 119. This is the longest chapter in the Bible, with 176 verses, and contains a wealth of descriptions and promises to those who choose to follow God's Word.

C. Scripture Memory Verse for the Week

Try to write your Scripture verse for the week from memory.

_____

_____

_____

DAY FOUR: HOW SHOULD WE STUDY THE BIBLE?

There are various methods and directions that you can use for studying the Bible. For instance, there are character studies, where you take the life of a biblical character and examine the events and substance of his or her life in detail. There are thematic studies, where you take a theme from the Bible and follow it through the different books. There are doctrinal studies, where you take the primary doctrines of Scripture and explore passages of the Bible concerning those doctrines. There are also book studies, key text studies and inductive studies...the list goes on. However, there are some common elements in every method of Bible study that you need to understand.

A. Three Crucial Areas in Studying the Bible

The Scripture below gives three crucial areas that must be included in every method of Bible study:

> *"They read from the book, from the Law of God, clearly, and they gave the sense, so that the people understood the reading."*
>
> (Nehemiah 8:8)

Read from the Book of the Law of God

The first step in proper Bible study is the *presentation*. We cannot hope to understand the Scripture until we first begin to read it. The presentation of Scripture is mandatory for a proper understanding. This may seem simple, but there are many who would prefer not to read the Bible and instead allow others to dispense God's Word to them.

Read Acts 8:30. What did Philip hear the Ethiopian eunuch doing?

_____

_____

_____

What question did Philip ask?

_____

_____

_____

It is important to have a *hunger for personal Bible study.* Read Acts 17:11. What two things made the Bereans nobler in character than the Thessalonians?

1. _____

2. _____

Make It Clear

The second step in proper Bible study is known as the *explanation.* There are times when we will come to a passage of Scripture that is more difficult than others. In these instances, God provides several channels that we can take to help gain understanding.

Read Acts 8:34-35. How did God bring clarity to the Ethiopian?

_____

_____

_____

Note that God often uses *explanation through others.* Read Acts 18:26. What two people did God use to help bring a greater understanding to Apollos?

1. _____

2. _____

We can also receive explanation *directly from God.* Read Philippians 3:15-16. Who is it that should take "such a view of things"?

_____

_____

_____

If we think differently than what the Word has said, what will God do?

_____

_____

_____

Until then, what should we do?

_____

_____

_____

Gave the Sense so that the People Understood

This third—and perhaps most diffi cult—step is known as *application*. It is a foolish thing to think that we can come to an understanding of the Word of God and not be held accountable to obey it. The Scripture is not meant to just be studied but also to be applied.

Read Acts 8:36-37. What evidence does this passage give that indicates the Ethiopian wanted to apply the Word of God when he finally understood it?

_____

_____

_____

Read James 1:22-25. Finish the sentence from James 1:22:

"But be doers of the word..." _____

_____.

What do Christians do to themselves if they only listen to the Word of God without obeying it?

_____

_____

_____

In verse 25, what is the promise for those who apply the Word of God?

_____

_____

_____

B. Summarizing the Matter

What are the three necessary areas of personal Bible study that should be included in all methods of studying the Word of God?

1. _____ Reading the Bible for yourself

2. _____ Gaining understanding through instruction

3. _____ Doing what the Bible says

C. A Final but Most Important Step

One of the most forgotten aspects of personal Bible study is prayer. Prayer is a crucial part of coming to the Scriptures to gain wisdom for living. This is God's Word, and for us to understand it, we must come to God and ask for His direction and guidance. The Holy Spirit guides us into all truth (see John 16:13), and we cannot know the mind of God apart from the Spirit of God (see 1 Corinthians 2:11). Thus, it is crucial that we begin all Bible study with prayer.

Read James 1:5. How do we gain wisdom?

_____

_____

_____

How does God grant wisdom to those who ask?

_____

_____

_____

DAY FIVE: WHAT'S WITH MEMORIZING SCRIPTURE?

If the greatest resource available for the Christian life is the Word of God, it only stands to reason that we take God's Holy Word into our memory. One fantastic example of the power of Scripture memory is the time when Jesus was being tempted in the wilderness by the devil (see Matthew 4:1-10). As Satan tempted our Lord, the only rebuttal and defense that Jesus offered came from the Word of God. Jesus quoted Scripture to answer every temptation that came His way, and as His followers, we need to be able to do the same.

A. Why We Should Memorize Scripture

The only way to ensure the Word of God is available to us at all times is to put it to memory. Let us take a look at some reasons why we should memorize Scripture.

Memorizing Scripture Provides Tools for the Holy Spirit to Work in Our Lives

One of the realities of the Christian life is that the Holy Spirit of God dwells within us and enables us to achieve God's will. One of the tools necessary for the Holy Spirit to work in us is God's Word.

Read John 14:26. What are two of the functions of the Holy Spirit?

1. _____

2. _____

What is necessary for us to possess before we can be *reminded* of something?

_____

_____

_____

Memorizing Scripture Enables Us to Overcome Sin

We all face many temptations in life. God has provided a means of dealing with and overcoming every sin that assails us.

Read Psalm 119:11. What does it take to keep a person from sinning against God?

_____

_____

_____

Note: Memorizing the Word of God will not ensure total success as a Christian, but not having Scripture in your heart just might guarantee total failure.

B. How We Should Memorize Scripture

One way in which we memorize Scripture is by meditating on God's Word. Meditation is more than sitting in some crossed-leg position chanting mantras. Meditating on the Word of God exposes your life to the glaring light of truth with the intention of changing your life to become more like Christ.

Read Joshua 1:8. What is the purpose of meditation?

To do all that written. Will make your way prosperous and have good success

What are the results that come from obedient meditation of God's Word?

Read Psalm 1:2. Why should we meditate on God's Word?

It is our delight

C. When We Should Memorize Scripture

One key element to successful Scripture memorization is to make it a daily habit. There is no way for a person to hide the Word of God in his or her heart if that person does not do it on a daily basis. One reason that you know phone numbers, names, addresses and other pertinent information is because you are constantly using them. Scripture memorization is no different.

Constant Use Gains Success

Spiritual maturity is gained through constant use of Scripture. Read Hebrews 5:14. For those who are trying to memorize Scripture, what is gained by constantly pursuing it?

ability to distinguish between good and evil. Spiritual discernment

Daily Habits Promote Good Memorization

Those who delight in Scripture will do what it takes to know it. Read Psalm 1:2-3. How often should a person meditate on the Bible?

Day and night

What does a person who makes the Bible a daily meditation become like?

a tree planted by streams of water that yields fruit in its season. Connected to source (word/water)

What three things happen to those who delight in the Word of God?

1. *yields fruit - witness to others*
2. *leaf does not wither — stay strong*
3. *prosper*

D. Scripture Memory Verse for the Week

What is your Scripture memory verse for the week? Write it below.

DAY SIX: TIME FOR REVIEW

Below are five review sections, one for each day. Try to do them without referring back to the lesson. Recheck your work and bring any questions you have to class.

Day One

How many books comprise the Old Testament, and approximately when were they written?

_____

_____

_____

What are the names of the first and last books of the Old Testament?

1. _____

2. _____

Day Two

How many books comprise the New Testament, and approximately how many authors wrote them?

_____

_____

_____

What are the names of the first four books of the New Testament?

1. _____

2. _____

3. _____

4. _____

Day Three

What three things will the study of the Word of God do in a believer's life?

1. _helps us grow_
2. _changes us_
3. _delivers us_

Day Four

What are three necessary elements of personal Bible study?

1. _read the Bible_
2. _Understand it_
3. _Obey it_

Day Five

What two reasons are given in the Bible for Scripture memorization?

1. _to be a tool for the Holy Spirit_
2. _overcomes sin_
3. _____

Memory Verse

Write your Scripture verse for the week from memory.

_____

_____

_____

CHAPTER 3

SALVATION AND ASSURANCE— GOD'S PLAN FOR MANKIND

Memory Verse: *"For God so loved the world, that he gave his only Son, that whoever believes in him should not perish but have eternal life."*

(John 3:16)

AS WE BEGIN exploring what it means to be a Christian, it is important to understand the nature and purpose of God's salvation. At this point in our faith, many of us are still working through what it means to be saved—the most we know is that we've responded to the call for repentance and have come into a relationship with Jesus, trusting our lives to Him. Well, that, in a nutshell, is salvation. This week's study will dive into a greater understanding of God's work in salvation, mankind's need for salvation, the nature of salvation, why a Christian should be baptized, and how to know for certain that we're saved.

DAY ONE: GOD'S WORK IN SALVATION

If you are a Christian, salvation is evidence that God has worked a mighty miracle in your life. God, in saving you, allows for no one else to gain the glory or the credit. You were not convinced by some clever scheme or great presentation as if the salvation of God was a multi-level marketing plan. In fact, as it has been said, "Anything a person can talk you into someone else can talk you out of." The fact is that no one person has ever come to know the salvation of God without God drawing that person to His Son. You didn't come to know Christ as Savior because *you* thought it was a good idea but because *God* thought it was a good idea.

"No one can come to me unless the Father who sent me draws him. And I will raise him up on the last day."

(John 6:44)

One truth that is necessary to understand is that salvation is of the Lord. It is of the Lord, by the Lord, and even *for* the Lord! Not one person in all of human history has been able to deliver himself or herself from sin and be found pleasing in God's sight based upon his or her own righteousness. God has done a great work, and God alone gets the credit. Today, we are going to look at God's work in the salvation of mankind.

A. The Promise of Salvation Is Given

In God's love and desire for the redemption of humanity, He gave His promise to provide a means of salvation for the entire human race. This promise is evident from the time of the fall of mankind in the Garden of Eden, throughout the Old Testament, and in the New Testament.

God Promises a Savior After the Fall of Man

Read Genesis 3:15. What promise is made concerning the destruction of the serpent?

The Serpent will be crushed

What do you think it means when God says that the woman's offspring will crush the head of the serpent?

Jesus will defeat satan

What do you think it means when God says that the serpent will strike the heel of the woman's offspring?

Satan will be able to wound us

Promised Through the Prophets

Read Isaiah 7:14. What promise is given through the prophet Isaiah concerning Jesus? Look up Matthew 1:18 and see how it is fulfilled.

God will give a sign - Jesus birth

B. The Process of Salvation Begins

God had begun the process of salvation from eternity past. Even at the fall of man in the Garden of Eden, God had started the process through which He would redeem the human race.

God Drives Humans Out of the Garden of Eden

Read Genesis 3:22-24. Why do you think God send Adam and Eve out of the Garden of Eden?

What would have happened if the man and woman were allowed to eat of the tree of life?

How do you think this demonstrates God's process of salvation?

The Plan of Salvation Before Creation

Read 1 Peter 1:20. When did God choose to send His Son into the world for the redemption of mankind?

He was foreknown before the foundation of the world. came in human form for our sake

C. The Power of Salvation Displayed

God has revealed the power for salvation in the resurrection of Jesus, His only Son. As Paul states in 1 Corinthians 15:17, "And if Christ has not been raised, your faith is futile and you are still in your sins." Without the resurrection of Jesus, there is no salvation!

God's Power Revealed in Scripture

Read Romans 1:16. The gospel is the power of God for whom?

power of God for all who believe Jew first and then the Greek

Read 1 Corinthians 1:18. For those who are perishing, what is the message of the gospel?

Folly to those who are perishing and the power of God to those who are saved.

D. The People of Salvation Chosen

God knows people's hearts and who will believe upon Him for eternal life. All who have believed have been chosen in Christ to receive the salvation of God.

The Many and the Few

Read Matthew 22:14. How many are invited to receive salvation?

_____

_____

How many are chosen?

_____

_____

_____

Where the Chosen Come From

Read John 15:19. From where does Christ choose those who will follow Him?

_____

_____

_____

If Christ has chosen us, do we belong to the world any longer? Why or why not?

_____

_____

_____

Chosen with a Purpose

Read 1 Peter 2:9. What is the purpose for which Jesus has chosen us out of the world?

_____

_____

_____

What are the four characteristics of the people whom Jesus calls?

1. _____

2. _____

3. _____

4. _____

DAY TWO: THE CONDITION OF MAN

Since the time of the fall of mankind at the rebellion in the Garden, all of humanity has lived in a state of separation from and disobedience toward God. There is not one person among the whole of the human race who has, through his or her own righteousness, been able to please God. Even Abraham, who was called God's friend, needed to have God impart righteousness to him. Only Jesus has lived the perfect and God-pleasing life. Look at what Jeremiah says:

> *"The heart is deceitful above all things, and desperately sick; who can understand it?"*
>
> (Jeremiah 17:9)

Paul echoes this sentiment when he states in Romans 3:23, "For all have sinned and fall short of the glory of God." We must understand that there is no hope for the human race apart from Jesus.

A. Mankind Is Sinful from Birth

Every person born since the Fall of man, with the exception of the Lord Jesus, begins life as a sinner.

Sinful Before Awareness

Read Psalm 51:5. According to this passage, when does everyone become a sinner?

_____

_____

_____

Does a person have to do wrong things to have a sinful nature? Why or why not?

_____

_____

_____

Straying Even at Birth

Read Psalm 58:3. When do the wicked go astray?

_____

_____

_____

Read Romans 3:10. How many righteous people are there? What about you?

_____

_____

_____

B. Mankind Is Powerless to Change

There is not one person who, by his or her own efforts, can make himself or herself pleasing to God. For all of the great and noble deeds that are done, not one of them meets the righteous standard that God has set. Trying to please God with human righteousness is like washing a car with an oil rag. No matter how much effort is given to clean the car—no matter how much work is put into it—the car will remain filthy. All of our efforts to please God amount to nothing unless God Himself washes us.

A Timely Sacrifice

Read Romans 5:6. At what time does this passage say that Jesus died for us?

_____

_____

_____

What is the condition that Jesus found us in?

_____

_____

_____

Who did Jesus die for?

_____

_____

_____

Until we realize our powerlessness, the sacrifice of Jesus means nothing. As long as we think we can do something to save ourselves, Jesus' sacrifice is meaningless.

The Nature of Human Righteousness

Read Isaiah 64:6. What have all of us become like?

_____

_____

_____

What are our righteous acts like in the sight of God?

_____

_____

_____

C. **Mankind Does Not Seek God**

No one, without the prompting of the Lord, has ever sought to have a relationship with Jesus Christ. We, like sheep, have gone astray, and there is no one who truly seeks after God on his or her own. There may be those who seek to gain knowledge about God, but there is no one who seeks God Himself without God first prompting that person to do so.

Read Romans 3:11, and fill in the missing words below.

No one... _____   no one... _____.

Look back at your life and see if you can identify circumstances where God was drawing you to Him. If you need some assistance, talk with your class facilitator.

Who Loved First?

Read 1 John 4:10, 19. Who loved first? Did we love God and He responded, or did God love us and we responded?

_____

_____

_____

How did God demonstrate His love for us?

_____

_____

_____

D. Mankind Is Without Internal Hope

Those who live without Christ live without hope. Many such people live in a constant state of fear because they have no hope of what their future will bring. Without knowing if their future is secure, they live in a continuous state of despair because they don't know what is in store for them. Only Jesus can bring the security and hope that we need to press on in this life.

The Cause of Hopelessness

Read Ephesians 2:12. What is the main cause of hopelessness in a person's life?

_____

_____

_____

What are the five conditions of those who are lost?

1. _____

2. _____

3. _____

4. _____

5. _____

Death Without Hope

Read 1 Thessalonians 4:13-14. What is the hope for those who believe?

_____

_____

_____

Why do the "rest of men" grieve when someone dies?

_____

_____

_____

DAY THREE: THE NATURE OF SALVATION

So far in this week's study, we have seen the work of God in salvation and the condition of those who need salvation. Now, we will turn our attention to the very nature of salvation to discover the tremendous wonder of what God has done for us. The fact is that God does not want anyone to perish. God wants all people everywhere to come to know the saving grace of the Lord Jesus, the mercy that is found at the cross, and the power that is found in the resurrection.

> *"The Lord is not slow to fulfill his promise as some count slowness, but is patient toward you, not wishing that any should perish, but that all should reach repentance."*
>
> (2 Peter 3:9)

A. Salvation Is Available to Everyone

God does not want anyone to be apart from Him for eternity. However, although His salvation is available to all, it does not mean that all will come to experience the saving grace of God. Remember, "Many are called, few are chosen." No one who has given his or her life to Jesus and trusted in Him is excluded from God's salvation.

God's Grace Made Available

Read Titus 2:11. What does the grace of God bring?

_____

_____

_____

To whom did God make His grace available?

_____

_____

_____

The Call of Jesus

Read Matthew 11:28. Who did Jesus call to come to Him?

_____

_____

_____

What did Jesus promise to do for those who came?

_____

_____

_____

B. The Nature and Fullness of the Salvation of God

There are three aspects of the salvation of God. These three aspects, though not exhaustive in understanding the nature of God's salvation, are complete in that they encompass the entire life of an individual.

We Are Saved from the *Penalty* of Sin

Read Romans 6:23. What are the "wages" of sin?

_____

_____

_____

What is the gift of God through Jesus Christ?

_____

_____

_____

We Are Saved from the *Power* of Sin

Read Galatians 5:24. What takes place when people receive God's salvation and belong to Him?

_____

_____

_____

How much power does sin possess in a believer's life?

_____

_____

_____

We Are Saved from the *Presence* of Sin

Read Revelation 21:4-5. What four things will God remove that are caused by sin? List them below.

1. _____

2. _____

3. _____

4. _____

How is God making everything (verse 5)?

_____

_____

_____

Read Revelation 22:3. What will happen to the curse that God gave at the time of the fall of mankind?

_____

_____

_____

C. The Need to Profess Our Faith Publicly

It is said that Jesus died for us publicly, so we need to publicly profess our faith in Him. By nature, we do not truly believe in something unless we are willing to stand for it. Thus, if we say that we believe in Jesus, we will be willing and eager to let other people know.

Making a Verbal Declaration

Read Romans 10:9-10. What does it mean to "confess with your mouth?"

_____

_____

_____

Can a person confess with his or her mouth without ever telling another person what he or she believes? Why or why not?

_____

_____

_____

Not Being Ashamed

Read Mark 8:38. What does Jesus say will happen to those who are ashamed of being His?

_____

_____

_____

Read Luke 12:8. If we acknowledge Jesus before others, what will Jesus do?

_____

_____

_____

If we disown Jesus before others, what will Jesus do?

_____

_____

_____

What does this tell us about the importance of making our faith public?

_____

_____

_____

DAY FOUR: BAPTISM—TAKING THE NEXT STEP

After a Christian publicly confesses his or her faith in Jesus, the next step of obedience is to be baptized. Literally translated, to be "baptized" means to be submerged in water. It is derived from an ancient term that sometimes described the sinking of a ship. Although baptism does not save a person, those Christians who are not baptized find their walk with Christ hindered in many ways. Jesus gave us the ordinance of baptism for the express purpose of showing the world and the church that we desire to follow Him in everything.

> *"For as many of you as were baptized into Christ have put on Christ."*
>
> (Galatians 3:27)

A. Who Can Be Baptized?

There are many church groups that follow their own personal plan concerning those who can be baptized. Nevertheless, the Bible gives a clear understanding as to who can be baptized.

Read Acts 2:41. After Peter spoke to the crowds in Jerusalem on the Day of Pentecost, about 3,000 people received Jesus as their Savior. What was the one qualifying element that allowed those 3,000 to be baptized?

_____

_____

_____

What was the message that they accepted (Acts 2:38)?

_____

_____

_____

B. How Is a Person Baptized?

Again, many different church groups follow a variety of practices concerning the method of baptism. As explained previously, the term "baptize" means to fully submerse in water. All of the examples of baptism we find in Scripture employ only one method.

John the Baptist in the Jordan River

Read Matthew 3:13-16. What does it mean when it says that Jesus came "up out of the water"?

_____

_____

_____

Philip and the Ethiopian Eunuch

Read Acts 8:36-39. Why did Philip and the eunuch have to go down into the water?

_____

_____

_____

C. **What Does It Mean for a Person Who Is Baptized?**

As stated before, baptism is an expression of our obedience and willingness to follow Jesus in everything we do. The word "baptism" means to be totally submerged in water, but there is a symbolic meaning as well.

Baptism Is an Expression of Our Faith

Read Romans 6:3 and Colossians 2:12. What does baptism symbolize in these passages?

_____

_____

_____

Baptism Is Symbolic of Our Pledge to God

Read 1 Peter 3:21. According to this passage, what is baptism? What is it not?

_____

_____

_____

What really saves us?

_____

_____

_____

D. When Can A Person Be Baptized?

Finally, although some think it wise to send new Christians through a lengthy education process before they are baptized, Scripture illustrates that people should be baptized as soon as possible after they come to believe in the Lord.

Read the following passages:

- Acts 2:41: The 3,000 believers at Pentecost
- Acts 8:38: The Ethiopian Eunuch
- Acts 9:18: Saul of Tarsus
- Acts 19:5: The Ephesians

In each of the above, how much of a delay was there between the individuals' conversion and their baptism?

_____

_____

_____

Have you been baptized? If not, why not?

_____

_____

_____

DAY FIVE: GAINING ASSURANCE OF YOUR SALVATION

One of the most frustrating and often debilitating things to go through as a new believer is not "feeling" like you are a Christian. All too often, new Christians assume that they must not be saved because they have lost that feeling of exuberance and excitement that they knew when they first became a believer in Jesus. However, being a Christian is not a matter of feeling but of faith. We are not Christians because we feel that we are; we are Christians because we believe upon the Lord Jesus Christ and have been saved. In the following section, we will examine some handholds to help us understand that God wants us to have confidence in our relationship with Him.

"But these are written so that you may believe that Jesus is the Christ, the Son of God, and that by believing you may have life in his name."

(John 20:31)

A. How to Know for Sure

One of the greatest strengths we have as believers in Jesus is the knowledge that we belong to the Son of God. Having confidence in our relationship with Jesus is essential for us to grow and develop in our Christian life. Here are some ways to know for sure that we are saved.

The Word of God Gives Assurance

Read 1 John 5:13. To whom were these words written?

_____

_____

_____

Why were they written?

_____

_____

_____

The Discipline of the Lord Gives Assurance

Read Hebrews 12:5-8. Who does the Lord discipline?

_____

_____

_____

If hardship comes in our lives, what is the Lord doing?

_____

_____

If we were not disciplined, what would that tell us about our relationship with Jesus?

_____

_____

_____

Living As Jesus Did Gives Assurance

Read 1 John 2:5. How do we know that we are in Jesus?

_____

_____

_____

Read Titus 1:16. Can a person claim to be in Jesus yet not walk as Jesus did? Why or why not?

_____

_____

_____

B. Handholds of Faith

All of us need a little reminder now and again of what we have in Jesus. With all the troubles and temptations that come our way daily, a little reminder of who we are in Christ is necessary.

Life Without Fear of Condemnation

Read Romans 8:1. If Jesus doesn't condemn us, is there anyone else who can?

_____

_____

_____

Who can live without fear of condemnation?

_____

_____

_____

Life Without Fear of Compromise

Read Romans 14:4. As Christians, to whom are we ultimately accountable?

_____

_____

_____

Who gives us the strength to live without compromise?

_____

_____

_____

C. What If We Sin?

One of the greatest fears in a new believer's life is that if they sin, they will once again be condemned by God and face eternal judgment. God does not want us to sin, and He will convict and compel us to a righteous life. But does this mean that if we sin we will lose the salvation that He has given to us?

We Cannot Be Separated

Read Romans 8:38-39. According to this passage, what can separate us from the love of Jesus?

_____

_____

_____

We Can Be Cleansed

Read 1 John 1:9. If we sin against God, what must we do?

_____

_____

_____

If we confess our sin—that is, agree with God concerning it—what will He do?

_____

_____

_____

We Can Not Be Condemned by Our Own Hearts

Read 1 John 3:18-20. How do we know that we belong to the truth?

_____

_____

_____

If our hearts condemn us, then who is greater than our hearts?

_____

_____

_____

D. Who Really Keeps Us?

Salvation is more than just our being able to believe and hold on to Jesus for dear life. The strength of salvation is not in our ability to believe but in God's ability to keep us. It is not us hanging on to God, but God holding on to us.

God Is the Keeper of Saints

Read Jude 1:24. What is God able to do?

_____

_____

_____

How will God present us before His glorious presence?

_____

_____

_____

Jesus Saves Completely

Read Hebrews 7:25. Who is Jesus able to completely save?

_____

_____

_____

The Holy Spirit Is a Deposit

Read 2 Corinthians 1:21-22. What three things did God do when we were saved?

1. _____

2. _____

3. _____

Why has the Holy Spirit has been put into our hearts?

_____

_____

_____

DAY SIX: TIME FOR REVIEW

Below are five review sections, one for each day. Try to do them without referring back to the lesson. Recheck your work and bring any questions you have to class.

Day One

After the Fall of man in Genesis 3, what promise did God make concerning the sending of a Savior?

_____

_____

_____

How was the power of salvation displayed in the life of Jesus?

_____

_____

_____

Day Two

According to Psalm 51:5, when does a person become a sinner?

_____

_____

_____

Can a person become righteous on his or her own and please God? Why or why not?

_____

_____

_____

Day Three

For whom is salvation made available? What Scripture reference supports this claim?

_____

_____

_____

What are the three elements of salvation?

Saved from the _____ of sin.

Saved from the _____ of sin.

Saved from the _____ of sin.

Day Four

What is the purpose of baptism?

_____

_____

_____

How should a person be baptized?

_____

_____

_____

Day Five

What three things provide a believer with the assurance of salvation?

1. _____

2. _____

3. _____

Who is our Advocate before the Father if we sin?

_____

_____

_____

Memory Verse

Write out your Scripture verse for the week from memory:

_____

_____

_____

CHAPTER 4

DEVELOPING A LIFE OF PRAYER

> **Memory Verse:** *"Do not be anxious about anything, but in everything, by prayer and supplication with thanksgiving let your requests be made known to God."*
>
> (Philippians 4:6)

"TEACH US TO pray!" This was the cry of the first disciples in Luke 11:1. These 12 men had been with Jesus on a daily basis and knew what it meant to follow Him, yet the greatest facet of the life of Jesus that they wanted to learn was how to pray. Why? To answer that question, we have to look at what happened when Jesus prayed. When Jesus prayed, 5,000 people were fed in one setting from just five loaves and two fish. When Jesus prayed, Lazarus came forth from the grave after being dead for four days. When Jesus prayed, all of humanity had the opportunity for redemption. When Jesus prayed, there was power and a sense that something was about to happen.

So, what is prayer? Prayer is that wonderful communication we have with the Father, which He granted to us so that we could come into His presence. Prayer is not the means of developing ourselves but of developing the life of Christ in us. If we are to be like Jesus, we must be like Jesus in prayer. Along with the Bible, prayer completes the circuit of communication we have with God. Many people mistake prayer as a means of getting things for themselves when, in fact, prayer is the method God has given us to draw near to Him, gaining His wisdom and understanding and establishing His holiness and purpose in our lives.

The goal this week is for you to understand and begin to develop a personal life of prayer. We will examine the priority of prayer, the purpose of prayer, and the practice of prayer as well as how to establish a daily prayer time and recognize God's answers to our prayers. For the rest of the week, the primary focus will be on what is termed the "Lord's Prayer." This is the prayer that Jesus taught His first disciples to pray and how the Spirit of the Lord will teach us to pray. It is found in Matthew 6:5-15, which will be our primary text this week.

DAY ONE: THE PRIORITY OF PRAYER

The heart of a believer should echo Psalm 42:1-2, which states, "As a deer pants for flowing streams, so pants my soul for you, O God. My soul thirsts for God, for the living God. When shall I come and appear before God?" Every Christian should have a passionate desire to want to know God. It should be as high a priority in his or her life as breathing. And just as breathing is necessary to maintaining life, prayer is necessary to develop and grow in relationship with the Father. Today, we will look at three reasons why prayer in the life of a Christian should be a priority.

A. Prayer Is Commanded by God

In Matthew 5:5, Jesus says, "And *when* you pray." There is a distinct reason that Jesus used the word "when" and not some other word such as "if." Jesus' expectation was that His disciples *would* pray! Prayer should thus be a priority in our lives because it is God Himself who commands us to do it. It is imperative that we become a people who pray. Let us look at some Scripture passages that relate to this command to pray.

A Parable on the Priority of Prayer

Read Luke 18:1-8. In verse 1, what did Jesus say was the purpose of the parable?

_____

_____

_____

According to this passage, what is required of us when we pray?

_____

_____

_____

Why do you think that Jesus asks the question at the end of the text?

_____

_____

_____

How is persistence in prayer a reflection of faith?

_____

_____

_____

A Command to Pray

Read 1 Thessalonians 5:16-18. Fill in the missing words from the text:

Rejoice _____ ; pray_____; give thanks in _____, for this is the will of God in Christ Jesus for you.

How often should we pray?

_____

_____

_____

According to verse 18, why should we give thanks in all circumstances when we pray?

_____

_____

_____

B. Prayer Is Commended by God

If God's command to pray is not enough of a motivation for you, consider the fact that God has also promised good to those who pray. In Matthew 6:6 we read, "And your Father who is in secret *will reward you.*" Let us look at some of the rewards that come from a life of prayer.

We Are Delivered from Temptation

Read Matthew 26:41. What two things must believers do to keep from falling into temptation?

1. _____

2. _____

What is the condition of the spirit and the flesh?

Spirit _____

Flesh _____

We Experience the Power of God

Read James 5:16-18. What are the two qualities of the prayer of the righteous?

1. _____

2. _____

Who does James use as an example of the prayer of the righteous?

_____

_____

_____

What did he do?

_____

_____

_____

We Receive the Peace of God

Read Philippians 4:4-7. According to this passage, for what should we pray?

_____

_____

_____

What is the promise for those who pray? Fill in the missing words from verse 7.

And the _____ of God which surpasses all understanding, will _____ your hearts and your minds in Christ Jesus.

C. Prayer Is Complimentary with God's Word

What God has promised to do for those who pray is extensive. It requires that we study the Scripture to understand all that is available through prayer. Thus, prayer is complimentary with the Word of God. They go hand in hand.

The Word of God Must Be in Us

Read John 15:7. What are the two requirements for receiving what we ask for?

1. _____

2. _____

If we are in Christ and Christ's Word is in us, what do you think will be asked for?

_____

_____

_____

Obedience Is a Requirement

Read 1 John 3:22. What two things must we do to receive anything from God?

1. _____

2. _____

DAY TWO: THE PURPOSE OF PRAYER

In Matthew 6:5-15, we find the model prayer that the Lord taught His disciples to pray. This prayer, from verse 9 to verse 13, is not intended to be a rote prayer that we recite over and over but a model upon which we can build a lifetime habit of purposeful prayer. There are five distinctive qualities we will examine today concerning the nature of the Lord's Prayer and how we are to develop a purposeful prayer life based on those qualities.

A. We *Praise* the Father in Heaven

The Lord's Prayer begins with this statement in verse 9: "Our Father in heaven, hallowed be your name." The term "hallowed" is a term of praise, which means "holy" or "exalted." We are meant to praise the Father in heaven.

Some Examples of Praise

Read Psalm 66:1-4. According to verse 1, what should all the earth be doing?

_____

_____

_____

When was the last time you shouted with joy to God?

_____

_____

_____

In Psalm 92:1, what two things are described as being good?

1. _____

2. _____

B. We *Position* Our Lives to God

In Matthew 6:10, we read, "Your kingdom come, your will be done, on earth as it is in heaven." We need to align our lives to God through prayer so that we are in His will and are able to follow Him.

The Prayer of Moses

Read Exodus 33:13. What was Moses' request?

_____

_____

_____

What two things did Moses desire from knowing the ways of God?

1. _____

2. _____

C. We Seek *Provision* for Our Needs

In the Lord's Prayer, Jesus teaches us that God will provide for our needs if we ask of Him. In Matthew 6:11 we read, "Give us this day our daily bread." More often than not, we want God to give us today our monthly supply. However, God wants us to rely on Him *daily*. He will provide for us each day as we seek Him for our needs.

Do Not Worry About Tomorrow

Read Matthew 6:25-34. Rather than seeking after the things of the world, what two things are Christians supposed to be seeking after (see verse 33)?

1. _____
2. _____

What are some of the things that you have worried about? Have you brought them to the Lord in prayer? Why or why not?

_____
_____
_____

D. We Seek *Purity* in Our Daily Lives

In Matthew 6:12, Jesus says, "Forgive us our debts, as we also have forgiven our debtors." The purity of our lives is predicated upon the forgiveness of God. We cannot be pure if we are not forgiven, no matter how well we try to live our lives.

Confession Brings Cleansing

Read 1 John 1:9. According to this passage, what are we to do?

_____
_____
_____

What two attributes of God are listed in this verse?

1. _____

2. _____

What two things will God do for those who confess their sins?

1. _____

2. _____

E. We Seek *Protection* from the Enemy

Finally, in Matthew 6:13, we read these words from Jesus: "And lead us not into temptation, but deliver us from evil." If we do not have protection from God against the devil, we have no protection at all. God will not let those who stay near Him fall into temptation and the devil's trap.

The Prayer of Jesus

Read John 17:15. What was Jesus' prayer for His disciples?

_____

_____

_____

Protection from the Devil's Work

Read Luke 22:31-32. What did Satan ask to do?

_____

_____

_____

What was Jesus' prayer for Simon?

_____

_____

_____

What did Jesus expect Simon to do when he turned back to Jesus?

_____

_____

_____

DAY THREE: THE PRACTICE OF PRAYER

So far this week, we have seen that prayer is a priority because God has commanded it and that prayer has a purpose in the life of every believer. Today, we will examine some practical aspects of prayer that every Christian should practice. So much of our time is spent with so many different priorities that we often lose sight of the fundamentals of prayer. However, if we neglect the practice of prayer, like anything else, it will get lost in the myriad of other, less important priorities.

I remember one time being at a mission in Korea when a young Christian military man came in. He exclaimed proudly, "I just read the neatest book on prayer!" Without hesitation, the missionary spoke up and said, "That is about the next best thing." What the missionary meant is that no matter what we learn about prayer, if we do not practice it, that knowledge is useless. There are three aspects of the practice of prayer that we will discover today from our text in Matthew 6:5-15.

A. The Practice of Prayer Is *Secret*

Get alone with God! Go to a quiet place that is unencumbered by the noise of this world and find solace in the presence of God Almighty. Find a place where you can exhaust your heart to the living God and receive from Him the blessing of that wonderful communion. Of course, this does not mean that you shouldn't gather together with other believers for corporate prayer meetings with the church—those times are also necessary. Spending time in secret prayer builds a deep, personal relationship with the Father.

Instructions on Secrecy

Read Matthew 6:5-6. What did Jesus call those who prayed only to be seen by men?

_____

_____

_____

What do you think Jesus meant when He said that they have received their reward in full?

_____

_____

_____

What will the Father do for those who pray in secret?

_____

_____

_____

The Example of the Lord Jesus

Read Mark 1:35. When did Jesus find time for solitary prayer?

_____

_____

_____

_____

When will you find time during your day for solitary prayer?

_____

_____

_____

B. The Practice of Prayer Is *Sincere*

Our prayers are not to be a rote exercise in religious expressionism. Prayer needs to come from the heart, or it is useless. If we pray only because it is the thing to do and we do not sense the need for prayer or seek the dynamic presence of God in prayer, all we are doing is reciting some religious phrase that, to God, is just like the pagan babble that was called prayer. True believers are those who practice sincerity in their prayer lives.

Instructions on Praying Sincerely

Read Matthew 6:7-8. How did Jesus say the pagans prayed?

_____

_____

_____

Why did the pagans think God would hear them?

_____

_____

_____

Why shouldn't Christians pray like the pagans?

_____

_____

_____

Example from the Early Church

Read Acts 12:1-5. What had happened to Peter?

_____

_____

_____

What did the church do in response to Peter's dilemma?

_____

_____

_____

How do you approach difficult or troubling situations in your life?

_____

_____

_____

C. The Practice of Prayer Is *Submissive*

One of the greatest truths that all Christians need to come to grips with is that it is God who wills and acts according to His own good pleasure. We are no more in control than a passenger on a cruise ship. We can argue and tell the captain which way to go and what to do, but ultimately the captain steers the ship. Prayer is not about us changing the mind of God or trying to get Him to see things our way; prayer is about us finding the presence of God and seeking the heart of God so that we can submit to His will and His way.

Recognizing the Position of God

Read Matthew 6:9-10. How does Jesus tell us that we can relate with God? What name does He use for God?

_____

_____

_____

What is the position of God in your life?

_____

_____

_____

According to verse 10, whose will should we desire to see done?

_____

_____

_____

How should God's will be done on earth?

_____

_____

_____

How is God's will being done in your life?

_____

_____

_____

The Example of Jesus

Read Matthew 26:36-42. In verse 38, how was Jesus feeling as He went into the garden of Gethsemane to pray?

_____

_____

_____

Whose will did Jesus submit to as He prayed (verses 39 and 42)?

_____

_____

_____

When you are overwhelmed with trouble, how do you pray?

_____

_____

_____

DAY FOUR: ESTABLISHING A DAILY PRAYER TIME

In both the Old and New Testaments, a regular time of prayer was vital in order for people to have a functioning, vibrant and living relationship with God. Some examples of men who lived in a prayerful relationship with God include David, who said, "O LORD, in the morning you hear my voice; in the morning I prepare a sacrifice for you and watch" (Psalm 5:3); and Daniel, of whom was said, "He got down on his knees three times a day and prayed and gave thanks to his God" (Daniel 6:10b). Jesus is our greatest example of a prayerful life, as we see in Luke 6:12: "In these days he went out to the mountain to pray, and all night he continued in prayer to God." The apostle Paul, as well, devoted his life to prayer, as we read in Colossians 1:9: "And so, from the day we heard, we have not ceased to pray for you." Prayer is not just a necessary function of a religious life; it is the very breath from the soul of every believer. Prayer should be to the Christian as air is to the lungs; we should be filled continually in prayer.

The question is how you can develop a time of prayer every day as part of your Christian existence. The primary need is to make prayer a daily activity; thus, the solution is to set aside a specific period of time to pray when you will not be interrupted. Today's activity is intended to help you begin that time of secluded prayer. Many people question what it is that they should pray about. Below are some Scripture references to give you some guidelines on what to pray for. Remember the five purposes of prayer on day two of this week and pray through them. You can use this as a framework for your continued prayer life. I would also encourage you to keep a journal of your prayers to see the activity of God—and rejoice!

A. Prayer As a Time of Praise to God

Consider who God is and what He has done for you. To help you begin to praise the Lord, read through a psalm. Psalm 100 is a good place to start. Pray that psalm back to God in your own words and from your heart!

List two characteristics of God for which you can praise Him:

1. _____

2. _____

List two things that God has done recently in your life for which you can praise Him:

1. _____

2. _____

B. Prayer to Position Your Life to God's Will

Spend the next few moments addressing the issue of God's will in your life. Is God's will a priority for you? Do you desire to do His will? Bring your life into subjection to the authority of God.

Read Psalm 40:8 and Colossians 2:20. List two areas of your life that you want to bring in line with God's authority:

1. _____

2. _____

C. Prayer to Seek God's Provision

It is God's desire to provide for His children. However, in seeking God's provision, we do not come to Him with our divine shopping list. We must come to Him and be subject to Him in all things, including the area of our needs. Our seeking God's provision should spring from our seeking God.

Read Matthew 6:33 and Malachi 3:10. List two needs in your life right now that God must provide for or they will go unmet:

1. _____

2. _____

List two areas in your life that you need to show faithfulness to God in order for Him to provide:

1. _____

2. _____

D. Prayer to Seek Purity in Your Life

God's desire is for all His people to be holy. God wants us to live a life of righteousness and purity. Of course, there are times (sometimes every day) that we sin against the will of God and live contrary to His word; however, through prayer, God has given us a means to be renewed day by day and experience His cleansing.

Read 1 John 1:9 and Acts 3:19. List two sins that you must confess and repent of as God is seeking purity in your life:

1. _____

2. _____

List two areas where you need to seek the forgiveness of another as well as God:

1. _____

2. _____

E. Prayer to Seek God's Protection

God will defend His people! The temptations and difficulties that besiege our lives is greater than we can handle. We have no possibility of overcoming the struggle with the enemy of our souls if we do not seek the one who is our Rock and Redeemer.

Read James 4:7 and 1 Peter 5:8-11. List two areas where you sense the enemy has come against you:

1. _____

2. _____

List two areas where you need to submit to God to avoid the devil's trap:

1. _____

2. _____

These five areas are a good way to begin a journey of prayer with the Father. Later on, we will discover how to pray for those who are lost without Jesus, for leaders and those who are in authority, and for the specific needs of God's people.

DAY FIVE: RECOGNIZING GOD'S ANSWERS TO PRAYER

One of the most frequent questions that Christians ask is, "How do I know when God has answered my prayer?" In fact, we often relegate circumstances that take place as just coincidence rather than a direct answer to the prayers of God's people. The story of Peter's escape from prison in Acts 12 is a prime example of a church missing the answer to prayer when it was right before their eyes. In a nutshell, the church was praying for Peter, and God sent an angel to help Peter escape from prison. Peter went to the house where the church members had gathered for prayer, but when the servant girl announced that it was Peter at the door, they didn't believe her! In fact, they said that she was out of her mind!

We often look at the circumstances and forget that those circumstances are exactly what we have been praying for all along. In today's lesson, we are going to examine three requirements for our prayers to be answered. These will give us the confidence we need to keep on praying, because we know that God will answer His peoples' prayers if the right conditions are met.

A. We Pray in Accordance with God's Will

All prayers that God answers are in accordance with His perfect will. God will never violate His will, and He will never go against what He has already determined from the dawn of eternity. However, for us to be involved in the workings of God and be a part of His divine providence, we need to pray in accordance with His will. The first thing to do, then, is to understand what the will of God is so that we can pray correctly.

Understanding and Knowing the Will of God

Read Romans 12:2. What two commands are given in this passage?

1. _____

2. _____

What will be the result if these conditions are met?

_____

_____

_____

What three terms describe the will of God?

1. _____

2. _____

3. _____

Praying in the Will of God

Read 1 John 5:14-15. What promise do we have if we ask anything in accordance with God's will?

_____

_____

_____

What promise do we have if we know that God hears us?

_____

_____

_____

B. We Pray in Conjunction with Our Needs

God delights in meeting the needs of His people. Oftentimes when we pray, we receive no answer due to the fact that we are praying for our wants and not our needs. We must be in tune with God and realize that He sees things differently. Seeking God and asking for our needs to be met—provided it is truly our needs for which we are praying—will bring God's answer.

The Promise Concerning Our Needs

Read Philippians 4:19. Who is the one who will meet all of our needs?

_____

_____

_____

With what measure will God meet our needs?

_____

_____

_____

Failure to Have Our Prayers Answered

Read James 4:3. What keeps us from receiving answers to our prayers?

_____

_____

_____

What motives should we have as we petition God for our needs?

_____

_____

_____

C. We Are Obedient

God will act in accordance with our obedience. If we are disobedient, our prayers will go unanswered—even if we have legitimate needs and our prayers are in accordance with His will as revealed in His Word. This does not mean that we have to be perfect before our prayers will be answered, but God does expect that we will strive to live in obedience.

God's Word Must Abide Within

Read John 15:7-10. What does it mean to abide in Christ?

_____

_____

_____

How does the word of Christ abide in us?

_____

_____

_____

What is the promise we are given if we are obedient to the Word of God?

_____

_____

_____

DAY SIX: TIME FOR REVIEW

Below are five review sections, one for each day. Try to do them without referring back to the lesson. Recheck your work and bring any questions you have to class.

Day One

What are three reasons why every Christian should make prayer a priority?

    1. _____

    2. _____

    3. _____

Day Two

What are the five purposes of prayer?

    1. _____   4. _____

    2. _____   5. _____

    3. _____

Day Three

What three elements should be found in our practice of prayer?

    1. _____

    2. _____

    3. _____

Day Four

Write out at least one (if not more) answers to the prayers that you prayed for this day.

_____

_____

_____

Day Five

What three conditions must be met for our prayers to be answered?

1. _____

2. _____

3. _____

Memory Verse

Write out your Scripture verse for the week from memory:

_____

_____

_____

CHAPTER 5

CHURCH DYNAMICS

> **Memory Verse:** *"And they devoted themselves to the apostles' teaching and the fellowship, to the breaking of bread and the prayers."*
>
> (Acts 2:42)

THIS WEEK WE are going to examine one of the most misunderstood realities of Christian living: church dynamics. It has been suggested by some that a person does not need to attend or belong to a church to be a Christian. This is true; however, it is downright impossible to be an effective or growing Christian if you are not part of a church. There is more to church than attending on Sunday morning and a casual Bible study once each week. The church is God's vehicle for the presentation of the gospel and the salvation of mankind. Jesus Christ died so that the church could be born, and He was resurrected so that the church could live!

Before we begin the week, we need to understand that Jesus is the head and foundation of the church. Ephesians 1:22 states, "God placed all things under his feet and appointed him to be head over everything for the church." Colossians 1:18 says, "He is the head of the body, the church; he is the beginning and the firstborn from among the dead, so that in everything he might have the supremacy." Ephesians 2:19-22 enjoins:

> So then you are no longer strangers and aliens, but you are fellow citizens with the saints and members of the household of God, built on the foundation of the apostles and prophets, Christ Jesus himself being the cornerstone, in whom the whole structure, being joined together, grows into a holy temple in the Lord. In him you also are being built together into a dwelling place for God by the Spirit.

As believers in Jesus, we need to become everything that He has desired for us. That will only happen when we are in the church.

DAY ONE: WHY THE CHURCH EXISTS

God does nothing apart from His purpose and desire, and the development of the church is no different. When God designed the church, He did so with four basic purposes in mind: *worship, fellowship, discipleship* and *membership.* These four purposes are found in His Word and were revealed to us to so that they could become the very foundation for His people.

A. The Church Exists to Glorify God Through Worship

One of the truths of the Christian life is that God calls us to become His worshipers. In fact, that is exactly what God is looking for: people who will worship Him. What worship means, in its simplest definition, is to attribute great worth to God. Worship has been described as "worth-ship." We are to look to God for who He is and what He does and give Him glory.

God Is Looking for Worshipers

Read John 4:23-24. Who is the object of our worship?

_____

_____

_____

What are the two criteria for true worshipers of God?

1. _____

2. _____

Called for a Purpose

Read 1 Peter 2:9. What has God called us to do?

_____

_____

_____

B. The Church Exists to Support One Another in Fellowship

The church is designed to support and encourage one another. God has brought us together to be a family and to function in the parameters of love for one another. The

Church should be the one place where a believer can find true and unselfish compassion and caring.

Committed to One Another

Read Hebrews 10:24-25. In verse 24, we are given a command. What are the two parameters of that command?

1. _____

2. _____

In verse 25, we are given the directives to fulfill that command. What are the two parameters to this?

1. _____

2. _____

What reason are we given in verse 25 for this directive from God?

_____

_____

_____

Demonstrated Fellowship

Read Acts 4:32. What demonstration of fellowship was found in the early church?

_____

_____

_____

C. The Church Exists for Discipleship

Jesus expects us to grow in the grace and knowledge of Him. We are to become better Christians today than we were yesterday. That process of growth is called "discipleship." A disciple is simply a follower or learner. John the Baptist had disciples, the Pharisees had disciples, and Jesus has disciples. All Christians are disciples of Jesus.

Growing to Become Like Jesus

Read Ephesians 4:15. Into whom are we to grow up?

_____

_____

_____

In how many things are we to become like Jesus?

_____

_____

_____

Leaving Behind Immaturity

Read Hebrews 6:1a. Finish the verse:

Therefore let us leave the elementary doctrine of Christ and _____

_____ .

D. The Church Exists to Reach the Lost

The goal of any growing organism is reproduction. We are meant to reproduce the grace of our Lord Jesus in the lives of those who have never given their lives to Christ. Proverbs 11:30 says that whoever wins souls is wise. We are to be wise in our Christian life.

What Jesus Makes Us Into

Read Matthew 4:19. When we follow Jesus, what does He make us into?

_____

_____

_____

The Apostle Paul's Example

Read 1 Corinthians 9:22. Finish the verse:

To the weak I became weak, that I might win the weak. I have become _____

to all _____ that by all _____ I might

save _____.

Do you consider your life to be a tool for God to bring salvation to another person? Why or why not?

_____

_____

_____

DAY TWO: GOD'S PERSPECTIVE OF THE CHURCH

Many people have an idea as to what the church should be. Some think that the church should be a social group. Others look at the church and want it to become a political activist organization. Some think that the church should just shut up and mind its own business. Some think that belonging to the church is a means of financial security; others think of it as a means to financial poverty. The world has one perspective of the church, while religious people have another. However, it is God's perspective that matters most. How does He see the church?

A. The Church: Universal and Local

The church, by God's unique design, is both universal (a global enterprise) and local (a congregation of local Christians). Just as we have an immediate family and an extended family, so in the church we have an immediate family (local) and an extended family (universal).

The Church Universal

Read Hebrews 12:23a. What is the name given to the church?

_____

_____

_____

Where are the records kept as to who truly belongs to the church?

_____

_____

_____

The Church Local

Read Colossians 4:15-16. According to verse 15, where did the church meet?

_____

_____

_____

The church at Colossae constituted one church. What other church is named in this passage?

_____

_____

_____

B. The Church: A Body of Believers

A hand and a foot, though different in function and form, belong to the same body. In the same way, the church, though it consists of different individuals, belongs to the same body of believers.

The Body of Christ

Read Ephesians 5:30. Of what are we members?

_____

_____

_____

Diverse Yet United

Read 1 Corinthians 12:12-13. How did Christ bring us together as one body?

_____

_____

_____

C. The Church: The Bride of Christ

Not only are we the body of Christ, but we are also considered the bride of Christ. God has called us to be united to Jesus as closely as a husband is united to his wife. We are to be so related to Jesus that we know Him intimately.

Set Apart for Jesus

Read 2 Corinthians 11:2. According to this passage, how are we set apart?

_____

_____

_____

How are we to be presented to Jesus?

_____

_____

_____

The Wedding of Christ and the Church

Read Revelation 19:6-8. In verse 8, what does "fine linen" represent?

_____

_____

_____

D. The Church: Children of God

Finally, we are called the very children of God. We have been adopted into the family of Jesus through our faith in Him. We are heirs of God and co-heirs with Christ and will be included at the "family reunion" at the end of the ages. Our names are already on the guest list called the Lamb's Book of Life.

The Spirit of Sonship

Read Romans 8:15-16. How, by the Spirit, are we able to address God?

_____

_____

_____

Who confirms that we belong as children of God (verse 16)?

_____

_____

_____

The Great Love of God for Us

Read 1 John 3:1. What prompted God to call us His children?

_____

_____

_____

Why doesn't the world know us?

_____

_____

_____

Day Three: Four Areas of Church (and Personal) Growth

For this study today, we are going to use the example of Jesus and His growth as seen in Luke 2:52: "And Jesus increased in wisdom and in stature and in favor with God and man." One thing is certain: God expects His church to grow. Christians who are in churches where growth is not talked about or expected are in a stunted and handicapped church. Our physical bodies are expected to grow, and when they don't, we go to the necessary medical professional to assess what is wrong and try to correct the situation. The same is true for the spiritual body of Christ. From the example of Jesus, we are going to see four areas for defining growth that should be taking place in the church today

A. Wisdom: Growth Through Discipleship

We as Christians should desire to know Jesus more and more. Paul the apostle expressed this in Philippians 3:10, "That I may know him and the power of his resurrection and may share in his sufferings, becoming like him in his death." The goal of our lives is to become like Jesus. That is the reality of discipleship.

The Goal of Our Efforts

Read Colossians 1:28. Who do we proclaim?

_____

_____

_____

Whom do we admonish and teach?

_____

_____

_____

What is the goal of this effort?

_____

_____

_____

The Revelation of God's Wisdom

Read 1 Corinthians 2:6-12. What is the wisdom of which we speak (verse 7)?

_____

_____

_____

How has God revealed this (verse 10)?

_____

_____

_____

Who allows us to understand what God has freely given us?

_____

_____

_____

B. Stature: Growth in the Membership

As families grow through the birth of children, so the church must grow through the birth of new believers. Jesus told Nicodemus that no man enters into God's kingdom unless that man is "born again." It is this new birth that Christians need to be pursuing as they share the gospel with those who are lost.

Ambassadors of Christ

Read 2 Corinthians 5:20. As ambassadors of Christ, what is God doing through us?

_____

_____

_____

What appeal is being made?

_____

_____

_____

Growth God's Way

Read Acts 2:47b. Who is it that adds to the church daily?

_____

_____

_____

How are new believers added to the church?

_____

_____

_____

C. Favor with God: Growth in Worship

Our lives should be a continual expression of devotion to Jesus in everything we do. We should strive to worship Jesus in every situation. Worship is not just what we do on Sunday morning as we sing songs to God. Worship is living out our lives to please the Lord because of our love for Him.

Instructed How to Live

Read 1 Thessalonians 4:1. We are instructed how to live in order to do what?

_____

_____

_____

According to this passage, should you ever *stop* trying to please the Lord more? Why or why not?

_____

_____

_____

A Sacrifice of Worship

Read Romans 12:1. What is considered the offering of our bodies as living sacrifices?

_____

_____

_____

Why should we offer ourselves as a living sacrifice?

_____

_____

_____

D. Favor with Others: Growth in Fellowship

It has been said that if we don't grow together, we don't grow at all. If one part of a person's physical body were to grow while the others stayed the same, it would distort that person's body and hamper its effectiveness as a whole. We all must be growing together, both in our relationship to Jesus and in our relationships to one another.

Make the Effort

Read Romans 14:19. For what two things should we be striving?

1. _____

2. _____

What kind of effort should we be trying to make in order to achieve peace and mutual edification?

_____

_____

_____

Look Out for Each Other

Read Philippians 2:4-5. Whose interests should we be looking out for?

_____

_____

_____

Whose attitude should we adopt as our own?

_____

_____

_____

DAY FOUR: OUR RESPONSIBILITIES IN THE CHURCH

As Christians, we are to take responsibility in the church. We only grow if we grow together, and we only grow if each part does its work. If your leg decided that it was tired of carrying you around and decided to quit functioning, you would be in serious trouble. In the same way, if one member of the body of Christ chooses not to function, the Church as a whole is in serious trouble. Just as the physical body must compensate for the loss, so must the spiritual body. As citizens of God's kingdom and members of the body of Christ, we must do the work that we have been given. Although no one can tell a person what his or her specific assignment is, there are some basics that all believers must recognize.

A. We Must Be Available for the Work

God wants us to be doing the things that Christ did while He was on the earth. We need to set ourselves apart for the tasks that we are called to do.

Created by God for Good Works

Read Ephesians 2:10. Whose workmanship are we?

_____

_____

_____

Why were we created in Christ Jesus?

_____

_____

_____

Who placed those works there in the first place?

_____

_____

_____

The Surrendered Life

Read Romans 12:1. What are we to do with our bodies?

_____

_____

_____

B. We Are to Hold Each Other Accountable in the Work

This doesn't mean that we are to look down on someone who is struggling and fighting just to make it through the day. To hold someone accountable means to come alongside that person and help him or her on the journey until that person can carry his or her own load.

Confession Is Good for the Soul

Read James 5:16. What is the purpose of confessing our sins to one another?

_____

_____

_____

A Life of Encouragement

Read Hebrews 3:13. How often should we encourage one another?

_____

_____

_____

What is the goal of encouraging others?

_____

_____

_____

C. We Are to Support the Work with Our Resources

There are three areas of life that comprise all of the assets we possess: our time, our talents, and our treasures. If we are to dedicate our lives to the service of God and the work He calls us to do, we must surrender each of these areas of our lives to Him.

Surrendering Our Time

Read Ephesians 5:15-16. How should we live our lives?

_____

_____

_____

What should we do with every opportunity? Why?

_____

_____

_____

Surrendering Our Talents

Read Colossians 3:23-24. How are we to do our work for the Lord?

_____

_____

_____

Who are we working for—the Lord or men?

_____

_____

_____

What is the reward?

_____

_____

_____

Surrendering Our Treasures

Read 2 Corinthians 9:6-7. Complete the verse:

The point is this: Whoever sows _____ will also reap _____,
and whoever sows _____ will also reap _____.

According to verse 7, whom does God love?

_____

_____

_____

D. We Are to Become Usable to Do the Work

We must become useful to the Master. Although it is God who changes us to be like His Son, we must also develop the life of Christ within us. Using the body as an illustration, God has given us the muscles and ability to develop and strengthen our physical form. In Christ, we have been given everything we need for life and godliness. Now we must take the initiative to strengthen what is in us; namely, the life of Christ.

An Instrument of Noble Purposes

Read 2 Timothy 2:20-21. There are four distinct descriptions given in this passage of the person who cleanses himself or herself. List them below.

1. _____

2. _____

3. _____

4. _____

Standing on the Promises

Read 2 Corinthians 7:1. Because of God's promises, what should we do?

_____

_____

_____

What is the result of purifying ourselves?

_____

_____

_____

DAY FIVE: REASONS FOR CHURCH MEMBERSHIP

As stated previously, some people have argued that belonging to a local church is insignificant and not a necessary part of the Christian experience. Again, I would say that those who do not belong to a local church are stunting their own Christian growth and placing a barrier in the path that God has called them to walk. We need to understand some basic reasons why church membership is important and why we should belong to a local body of believers. Today, we are going to examine four reasons why belonging to a local church is important.

A. Belonging to a Church Shows that You Belong to Jesus

One key element of church membership is that it demonstrates a commitment to Christ. Jesus was committed to the church, as He demonstrated when He died for her. The apostles were committed to the local church, and thus the majority of the New Testament was written. Commitment to a local church is an indication of commitment to Christ.

We Belong to Each Other

Read Romans 12:5. To whom do we belong?

_____

_____

_____

Whose body are we?

_____

_____

_____

A Negative Illustration

Read 1 John 2:19. If the believers depicted in this verse really belonged to the church, what would they have done?

_____

_____

_____

What did their leaving the church demonstrate?

_____

_____

_____

B. Belonging to a Church Gives You a Place of Service

We all need a chance and a place to exercise our giftedness from God. Every believer is called to serve the Lord in some capacity. The church is where that service is to take place.

Administering the Grace of God

Read 1 Peter 4:10-11. Who do we serve when we use our gifts?

_____

_____

_____

Who is to be praised in the functioning of our gifts?

_____

_____

_____

Devoted to Service

Read 1 Corinthians 16:15. To what did the household of Stephanas devote themselves?

_____

_____

_____

C. Belonging to a Church Gives you Support

In the church, we find the strength and support that we need to continue in the life that God has placed before us. There will be difficulties and persecutions along the way, but when the church stands together, there is strength.

Help to Carry the Load

Read Galatians 6:2,10. What do we fulfill if we carry each other's burdens?

_____

_____

_____

When should we do good (verse 10)?

_____

_____

_____

To whom should we do good?

_____

_____

_____

D. Belonging to a Church Places You in the Path of God's Revelation

God reveals Himself through the church. He established the church on the foundation of the apostles' teachings, which we call the New Testament. He places shepherds in the church, whom we call pastors, to lead the body of Christ in accordance with God's Word. God's revelation comes through the church, and those outside are left virtually in the dark.

God's Wisdom Revealed

Read Ephesians 3:10. Through whom did God intend to reveal His wisdom?

_____

_____

_____

To whom did God intend to reveal His wisdom?

_____

_____

_____

Christ the Wisdom of God

Read 1 Corinthians 1:23-24. How do people outside the church see the crucifixion of Jesus?

The Jews: _____

The Gentiles: _____

How do people who have been called by Christ see the crucifixion?

1. _____

2. _____

DAY SIX: TIME FOR REVIEW

Below are five review sections, one for each day. Try to do them without referring back to the lesson. Recheck your work and bring any questions you have to class.

Day One

What are the four primary purposes of the church?

1. To glorify God through _____.

2. To support one another in _____.

3. To grow in our Christian life through _____.

4. To reach the lost and bring them in to _____ with Christ.

Day Two

List two of the four descriptions given for the church.

1. _____

2. _____

Whose perspective of the church matters most?

_____

_____

_____

Day Three

What are the four areas of church (and personal) growth?

1. _____

2. _____

3. _____

4. _____

Does God expect His church to grow? Why or why not?

_____

_____

_____

Day Four

What are the four responsibilities for Christians in doing the work of the church?

1. Be _____ for the work.

2. Hold each other _____ in the work.

3. Be _____ of the work.

4. Become _____ to do the work.

What are the three resources with which we support the work of the church?

1. _____

2. _____

3. _____

Day Five

What are the four benefits that those who belong to the church receive?

1. _____

2. _____

3. _____

4. _____

Memory Verse

Write out your Scripture verse for the week from memory:

_____

_____

_____

CHAPTER 6

STEWARDSHIP—
GAINING CONTROL OF LIFE

> **Memory Verse:** *"Moreover, it is required of stewards that they be found faithful."*
> (1 Corinthians 4:2)

WHEN PEOPLE TALK about stewardship, they usually focus on what people do with their money. Although the way in which we handle money is part of the biblical idea of stewardship, God is concerned not just with how we handle our money but also with how we handle our whole lives. This week, we are going to examine the biblical idea and method of gaining control of life.

Stewardship, by its very nature, is the way in which we take care of all the assets of life that God has given to us. Psalm 24:1 reads, "The earth is the LORD's and the fullness thereof, the world and those who dwell therein." Romans 14:8 states, "For if we live, we live to the Lord, and if we die, we die to the Lord. So then, whether we live or whether we die, we are the Lord's." Before we can even understand what proper stewardship is, we need to understand that God is the owner and sole proprietor of everything. Even the breath we breathe is given to us by God for us to use to His glory.

A steward is someone who is responsible to manage the resources of another. We are all stewards of what God has given us—and God has given us everything! God expects us to be faithful with everything we have because, ultimately, it all belongs to Him.

DAY ONE: CHOOSING THE STEPS OF OBEDIENCE

One of the great themes throughout Scripture is the call to choose between faithful obedience or selfish disobedience. The same is true of the manner in which God wants us to manage the assets of our lives. Furthermore, God gives us an understanding of what will transpire if we are faithful in obedience or if we are selfish in disobedience. For those who are faithful, blessings come; for those who are selfish, judgment comes.

A. Obedience or Selfishness

The question is not whether it is wise to be obedient but whether we are willing to be obedient. People know instinctively what the right and wrong choices are. How will we choose?

The Choice Between Serving God or Others

Read Joshua 24:14-15. What choice did Joshua place before the people of Israel?

_____

_____

_____

What choice did Joshua make for himself and his family?

_____

_____

_____

The Choice Between Two Masters

Read Luke 16:13. Can a person be devoted to two masters? Why or why not?

_____

_____

_____

How will a person react to having two masters?

_____

_____

_____

To what two masters does Jesus refer in this passage?

_____

_____

_____

Why do you think Jesus referred to money as being a master?

_____

_____

_____

B. Blessings Concerning Obedience

God always promises blessings for those who are obedient to Him. He always rewards those who are faithful to Him with the resources of their lives.

An Overflowing Blessing from Obedience

Read Malachi 3:8-12. How was the nation robbing God?

_____

_____

_____

What command did God give to His people?

_____

_____

_____

What would be the results if God's people were obedient?

_____

_____

_____

Faithfully Seeking After Jesus

Read Matthew 6:33. What two things are we to seek?

1. _____

2. _____

What is the result of seeking after God's kingdom and His righteousness?

_____

_____

_____

C. Judgments Concerning Selfishness

Just as there are blessings that come from obedience, there are judgments that come with disobedience. Disobedience, simply put, is selfishness. It is wanting to do things our way rather than God's way.

The Disobedient Stand Against God

Read 1 Samuel 12:15. What will happen to those who rebel against God?

_____

_____

_____

What do you think it means that God's hand will be against them?

_____

_____

_____

God's Wrath Comes upon the Disobedient

Read Ephesians 5:6. What method of deception is described in this verse?

_____

_____

_____

Upon whom does the wrath of God come?

_____

_____

_____

DAY TWO: STEWARDSHIP OF TIME

Of all the resources that we have, our time is the most precious to us. We can never earn time, save time, or stop using time—it is always marching on. There are only two ways in which we can spend our time: we can invest it or we can waste it. Every choice that we make is a determination of our priorities and how we address the time issue of life. We can use our time wisely and be productive, or we can use our time foolishly and squander it away and have nothing to show for it. We need to be conscious of what we are doing with our time and redeem the time that we have left to use for God's purposes and glory.

A. Spending Time Wisely

If you were to take an hourly calendar and keep a record of how you spent your time every day, what would be the end result? Do you invest your time, or do you waste it? To invest your time is to do those things that produce positive results that glorify God. To waste your time is to do those things that produce nothing.

Investing Your Time

Read Ephesians 5:15-16. How should we be careful to live?

_____

_____

_____

Why should we make the most of every opportunity?

_____

_____

Life Is Brief

Read James 4:14. Does anyone know what will happen tomorrow? Why or why not?

_____

_____

_____

What is life described as in this passage?

_____

_____

_____

Wasting Time

Read Proverbs 24:30-34. In verse 30, to what is the sluggard compared?

_____

_____

_____

What had happened to the field of the sluggard?

_____

_____

_____

In verse 34, what did the observer do?

_____

_____

_____

What happens to those who waste their time?

_____

_____

_____

B. Life: Choices at the Crossroads

Life is met at the crossroads of choice. Every decision that we make is based upon our priorities and our desires. If we want to use our time wisely, we must make our choices based upon the priorities of God and for the greatest results.

Choosing to Do the Right Thing

Read Matthew 24:45-51. What did the master give the servant to do?

_____

_____

_____

In verse 47, what was the servant's reward for choosing to do the work faithfully?

_____

_____

_____

What did the wicked servant think (verse 48)? What was his choice?

_____

_____

_____

What was the wicked servant's reward?

_____

_____

Do you have time to waste? Why or why not?

_____

_____

_____

C. Redeeming Time

What does it mean to redeem time? Consider this: what do you do when you redeem a coupon? You take the coupon to a retail store and trade it in for something that has value. Every day, you are trading in your time for the activities of your life. The question is whether those activities have any value. To redeem your time is to trade it in for that which has value. You cannot help but spend time—are you spending it on that which is useful?

Diligent or Lazy

Read Proverbs 13:4. What is the distinction between the sluggard and the diligent?

_____

_____

_____

Why do you think the desires of the diligent are fully satisfied?

_____

_____

_____

Imitate Those Who Left a Good Example

Read Hebrews 6:12a. Fill in the missing word from the text:

So that you may not be _____.

What two qualities do those whom we should imitate possess?

1. _____

2. _____

What is the reward of those who live their lives with faith and patience?

_____

_____

_____

DAY THREE: STEWARDSHIP OF TALENTS

All believers are gifted by God to serve Him and the church. All Christians have natural and spiritual talents that are to be used to bring glory to God. Although some Christians may think that they have nothing to offer the Lord in the way of service, God does not see it that way. God has given the Holy Spirit to every believer and promised that through Him we will have power to be witnesses for Jesus (see Acts 1:8). The Holy Spirit brings different gifts and abilities to each believer so that he or she can function within the body of Christ—the church. God then leads those who are faithful to Him to places and tasks that He has prepared in advance for them to do.

A. We Are Gifted to Serve

One of the greatest truths of Scripture is that when we were saved, God gifted us to serve. God expects that His people will become actively involved in the work of the kingdom of Heaven.

Gifted for the Common Good

Read 1 Corinthians 12:7-11. According to verse 7, for what purpose are the manifestations (gifts) of the Spirit given?

_____

_____

_____

According to verse 11, whose work is it?

_____

_____

_____

Who determines the giftedness of each believer?

_____

_____

_____

Good Works Are Put Before Us

Read Ephesians 2:10. Whose workmanship are we?

_____

_____

_____

What are we created to do?

_____

_____

_____

Who are we created in?

_____

_____

_____

Who prepared these works for us?

_____

_____

_____

B. Working Out What God Has Worked In

God created us for good works, and He has also put in us the ability to do those works. What we need to do is walk in faithfulness and use the gifts that we have been given to promote and advance the cause of Christ.

Obedience Is What Counts

Read Philippians 2:12-13. How does a person "work out" his or her salvation?

_____

_____

_____

Who is it that works in you?

_____

_____

_____

What two things does God work in you to do?

1. _____

2. _____

To whose pleasure do we work?

_____

_____

_____

C. Increasing Our Capacity for Service

One aspect of our Christian growth that often goes unspoken is that we can increase our own capacity for serving the Lord and become even more productive in the kingdom of Christ. We need to seek out ways of increasing our own capacity for fruitful service. Like a muscle, our giftedness will increase with use and decrease with neglect.

Preparing for Service

Read 2 Timothy 2:20-21. What are the articles in a large house, and what are their purposes?

_____

_____

_____

Four things describe a person who has cleansed himself or herself of dishonorable purposes:

1. _____

2. _____

3. _____

4. _____

Increase in Fruitfulness

Read John 15:2-3. What does the Father do to those branches that bear no fruit?

_____

_____

_____

What does the Father do to those branches that do bear fruit?

_____

_____

_____

For what purpose does the Father prune the fruitful branches?

_____

_____

_____

What tool does God use to prune the fruitful branch (verse 3)?

_____

_____

_____

DAY FOUR: STEWARDSHIP OF TREASURES

Jesus, in the four Gospels, spoke more about money than any other subject. It is important to understand that the way we handle our material possessions is a key indicator of the way we handle our relationship with Jesus. Jesus said that the master in competition with God is money (see Matthew 6:24). Paul says that the love of money is the root of all kinds of evil (see 1 Timothy 6:10) and that one of the signs of the end is that people will become lovers of money (see 2 Timothy 3:2). How we handle our finances and all our material possessions is vital to a growing relationship with Jesus.

A. Who Really Owns It?

God owns everything. From money to land to people, God is the creator and owner of all that there is. In fact, though people are clever and have the capacity to affect their environment, no one but God alone can truly create. Although we may use and manipulate this world, we cannot make something from nothing.

God Is the Owner of All Creation

Read Psalm 50:9-12. Is there anything that God does not own? What in this passage indicates that this is the case?

_____

_____

_____

Does God look to us to provide for Him? Why or why not?

_____

_____

_____

God Is the Owner of All Mankind

Read Ezekiel 18:4. What does this text say concerning the souls of men?

_____

_____

_____

If God owns even the souls of men, what happens to those who sin?

_____

_____

_____

B. **What Does God Expect from Us?**

If God is the owner of all things, then it stands to reason that He has some expectations concerning how we handle the things that we have. God has given us everything, including our very lives, to use according to His purpose. We need to look at everything we possess—from our money to our homes to our cars to our jobs to our very way of life—according to the expectations of God.

God Expects Us to Give What We Can

Read Mark 14:6-9. In verse 6, how did Jesus describe the gift that the woman gave?

_____

_____

_____

What did Jesus say concerning the woman's gift in verse 8?

_____

_____

_____

Do you do what you can in giving to Jesus?

_____

_____

_____

The Nature of Giving

Read 2 Corinthians 9:6-8. What happens to those who sow sparingly?

_____

_____

_____

What happens to those who sow generously?

_____

_____

_____

According to verse 7, how much should a person give?

_____

_____

_____

Who does this passage say that God loves?

_____

_____

_____

What is God able to do for those who give cheerfully?

_____

_____

_____

What is the result of God's grace abounding to us?

_____

_____

_____

C. To Whom Do We Really Give?

Some people think that when they give to a church, they are giving their money to support the pastor, keep the church's bills paid, or to advance a cause. However, the fact is that when we give our offerings, we are giving to the Lord. As we discovered, the Lord doesn't need our gifts, but He is looking for those who will be obedient and trust in Him.

The Example of David

Read 2 Samuel 8:10-11. To whom did King David dedicate the articles He received?

_____

_____

_____

Doing for Others Is a Gift to God

Read Matthew 25:31-40. What is the reward found in verse 34 for those who are faithful to give?

_____

_____

In verse 40, how does the king identify with those who received help?

_____

_____

_____

If you give to meet the needs of someone, to whom do you really give?

_____

_____

_____

DAY FIVE: COUNTING THE COST

One excuse people give for not being generous to the Lord and His purpose is because they cannot see that their generosity is going to do anything valuable. Such an attitude is an indication that they don't know the value of faithful obedience to God or the promises concerning those who are generous to the Lord. Those who think there is no value in giving to the Lord are not looking at it from God's perspective but from their own. God instructs us to count the cost of faithfulness and we need to look at stewardship in the same way. We need to count the cost of being a faithful steward and determine the importance of our stewardship. Today, we are going to examine the value of being a faithful steward of our lives.

A. The Value in Good Stewardship

There is tremendous value in being a faithful and generous giver. God has given incredible promises to those who are faithful in their giving. Consider some of the following.

The Generous Will Prosper

Read Proverbs 11:25. What is the promise given for those who bring a blessing?

_____

_____

_____

To "water" means to "refresh." So, who will be refreshed?

_____

_____

_____

God Will Be Generous in Return

Read Luke 6:38. If you give, what will be done for you?

_____

_____

_____

What four descriptions are given in this passage about how God will give back to those who are generous?

1. _____

2. _____

3. _____

4. _____

What measure will God use to give back to you?

_____

_____

_____

B. Opening the Door of God's Blessing

One thing is certain: God desires to bless His people. God is waiting for His people to be faithful so that He can throw open the gates of heaven and pour out the blessings that await those who are obedient.

The Floodgates of Heaven

Read Malachi 3:10-12. What is the requirement for God to throw open the floodgates of heaven?

_____

_____

_____

What is the size of the blessing that God promises to give to those who are obedient?

_____

_____

_____

According to verse 12, who will know that we have been blessed by God?

_____

_____

_____

C. Treasure in Heaven

The reality that our eternal home is in heaven is one that often goes unnoticed in the lives of God's people. We have a home waiting for us; thus, we should be storing up our treasure in heaven instead of storing it up here on earth. Although the treasures of heaven are not material but spiritual, they are found in the way we handle our material possessions here on earth.

Our Treasure in Heaven

Read Matthew 6:19-21. What happens to our treasures on earth?

_____

_____

_____

Can anyone take away our treasures in heaven?

_____

_____

_____

Finish the following from verse 21:

For where your _____ is there your _____ will by also.

The Method of Gathering Heavenly Treasure

Read 1 Timothy 6:18-19. What three things does Paul command us to do?

1. _____

2. _____

3. _____

In verse 19, what is the result of living a good and generous life?

_____

_____

_____

Day Six: Time for Review

Below are five review sections, one for each day. Try and do them without referring back to the lesson. Recheck your work and bring any questions you have to class.

Day One

What was the choice that Joshua gave to the people in Joshua 24?

_____

_____

_____

List two blessings that God gives to those who are obedient:

1. _____

2. _____

List two judgments that God gives to those who are selfish:

_____

_____

_____

Day Two

Why should we make wise use of our time?

_____

_____

_____

What does it mean to redeem our time?

_____

_____

_____

Day Three

Who gifts all believers to function in the body of Christ?

_____

_____

_____

What tool does God use to prune our lives for greater fruitfulness?

_____

_____

_____

Day Four

Who owns everything?

_____

_____

_____

When you give, to whom do you really give?

_____

_____

_____

Day Five

What is one promise that God gives to a person who is generous?

_____

_____

_____

According to Malachi 3, what will open the floodgates of heaven?

_____

_____

_____

Memory Verse

Write out your Scripture verse for the week from memory:

_____

_____

_____

CHAPTER 7

SHARING WHAT YOU BELIEVE

Memory Verse: *"For we cannot but speak of what we have seen and heard."*

(Acts 4:20)

ONE OF THE greatest hindrances to our walking faithfully with Jesus is our failure to share or talk about what has taken place in our lives. Often, one of the best-kept secrets in a Christian's life is the fact that he or she is truly a believer in Jesus. We were never meant to be saved and silent but saved and sharing what we believe. Consider this statement of Jesus in Matthew 10:32-33:

> So everyone who acknowledges me before men, I also will acknowledge before my Father who is in heaven, but whoever denies me before men, I also will deny before my Father who is in heaven.

This week, we are going to discover the essentials of sharing what we believe and the elements of a true and open testimony. Jesus expects us to be actively sharing our faith with a watching and desperate world. If we are unwilling to express what we believe and what has happened to us, there will be a multitude of people who will go to eternity without the hope of eternal life in Jesus. My prayer for you would be that of the apostle Paul in Philemon 1:6: "And I pray that the sharing of your faith may become effective for the full knowledge of every good thing that is in us for the sake of Christ."

One last thought to share with you: you have to run the risk of striking out to have the opportunity of hitting a home run. Don't ever think that people are going to just *see* you being a Christian and want to join together with Christ. People need to *hear* about your faith, and that requires you telling them. You will never get a hit unless you swing the bat, and you will never see a person saved unless you tell him or her about Jesus.

Day One: Essentials of Evangelism

Although not everyone is called to be an evangelist, everyone is called to evangelize. The word "evangelism" comes from the Greek word meaning to "preach the gospel." There are some basics of evangelism that every believer must understand in order to participate in reaching the world for Jesus. We are going to look at four essential elements for Christians to effectively evangelize.

A. Evangelize from a Heart of Conviction

It is true that people will speak with confidence about those things with which they are deeply convicted and convinced. When we speak about Jesus to those who don't believe, we must first be completely convicted that without Jesus everyone will perish. If we think that people have a chance at eternity without Jesus, we will never effectively share what we believe.

Speak According to What We Believe

Read 2 Corinthians 4:13. According to this passage, what should precede our speaking about Jesus?

_____

_____

_____

With what kind of spirit (inner conviction) should we speak?

_____

_____

_____

Speak from an Obedient Life

Read Acts 5:27-29. What orders did the Sanhedrin give to the apostles?

_____

_____

_____

What had happened in spite of the orders the Sanhedrin had given?

_____

_____

_____

In verse 29, what reason did the apostles give for their disobedience to the Sanhedrin?

_____

_____

_____

B. Evangelize Using the Necessary Elements of Communication

For us to effectively share the gospel, two elements of communication are necessary and must be in harmony with one another. Those who have these two areas of their lives in balance and harmony have a powerful testimony to a watching and listening world. These two areas of communication are visual communication and verbal communication.

Visual Communication Through a Righteous Life

Read Matthew 5:13-16. What two comparisons are made in this passage about a believer's life?

1. You are the _____ of the earth.

2. You are the _____ of the world.

What two analogies are made to believers being the light of the world?

1. A _____ set on a hill.

2. A _____ on a stand.

According to verse 16, what are those things that people will see in our lives?

_____

_____

_____

What will be the reaction of those who see our good deeds?

_____

_____

_____

Verbal Communication Through Speaking the Truth

Read Romans 10:14-15. There are four stages of communication listed in this passage. Each begins with, "How..." List below the four stages of communicating the gospel.

1. _____

2. _____

3. _____

4. _____

At which stage are unbelievers? At which stage should believers be?

_____

_____

_____

What praise is given to those who bring good news?

_____

_____

_____

C. Evangelize Using Foundational Elements of Content

Another important factor in evangelizing is the content of our communication. We must not take from or add to the message that has been given to us by God. God alone has set the parameters for what we are to say to others concerning the message of salvation, and if we are to be effective, we must remain within the framework of God's message.

The Message Given by Jesus

Read Acts 10:42-43. What were the apostles commanded to testify about?

_____

_____

_____

Who else has, in the past, testified about Jesus?

_____

_____

_____

What is the message that the prophets testified?

_____

_____

_____

The Priority of the Gospel

Read 1 Corinthians 15:1-8. Finish the Scripture passage from verse 1:

Now I would remind you, brothers, of the gospel I _____ to you, which you _____ in which you _____ .

Verse 2 states, "...and by which you are being saved." Is there any other gospel by which a person can be saved? Why or why not?

_____

_____

_____

What is the requirement of faith found in verse 2?

_____

_____

_____

In verse 3, what priority is the gospel?

_____

_____

_____

What are the three elements of the gospel found in verses 3 to 4?

     1. _____

     2. _____

     3. _____

To whom did Jesus appear after His resurrection?

_____

_____

_____

How has Jesus appeared to you? (Caution: this is a trick question!)

_____

_____

_____

D. Evangelize by Speaking to the Right Crowd

It is a wonderful thing to share with others of like faith the grandeur and majesty of God and how He has changed our lives. It is spiritual to do so and goes a long way toward encouraging and strengthening the family of believers. However, if we are to be successful in our evangelizing efforts, we must speak to the right crowd. The people who most need to hear the gospel are usually the ones with whom we are the most afraid to speak. We need to go to those who are not believers and share the wonderful truth of the gospel of grace found in Jesus.

Seen in the Ministry of Christ

Read Luke 19:5-10. With whom did Jesus go to be a guest? What was the reaction of the people?

_____

_____

_____

In verse 10, how did Jesus describe His ministry?

_____

_____

_____

Expressed in the Great Commission

Read Matthew 28:19. To which nations are we to go and make disciples?

_____

_____

_____

Read Acts 1:8. What three places are mentioned that we are to be witnesses?

1. _____

2. _____

3. _____

Do you know of anyone with whom the gospel of Jesus should not be shared?

_____

_____

_____

List one person below that you will pray for and commit to sharing the gospel with this week!

_____

_____

_____

DAY TWO: THE CALL TO SHARE

One of the most asked questions by believers is why they need to share what they have come to believe. After all, isn't religion a private matter? Doesn't everybody have the right to decide what to believe? Should we really force our religion on someone else? Can't we just live a Christian life—and that be good enough? All of these questions (and many others like them) have been asked down through the ages in the congregations of believers, but they all boil down to one simple question: why do we have to say anything at all? Today, we are going to look at three reasons why we must be active in sharing our faith. Keep your Bible open to Acts 1, as we will be using this text to springboard into our calling to share.

A. We Are Witnesses of the Person of Jesus

Every person who has been born again is a witness to the person of Jesus. Although we have not seen Him physically, His presence and activity are all around us and in us. His transforming power is on display in the lives of every obedient believer. Every person who has been touched by the saving power of Jesus has been given the responsibility to bear witness to the truth.

The Expression of a Transformed Life

Read 1 Peter 1:8-9. What are the two responses by those who know Jesus without physically seeing Him?

1. _____

2. _____

What is the result of such faith in Jesus?

_____

_____

_____

What is the goal of our faith?

_____

_____

_____

The Call to Be a Witness

Read Acts 1:8. What did Jesus say that we would be?

_____

_____

_____

Read Acts 4:20. To what two things does a witness testify?

1. _____

2. _____

B. We Are Commissioned to Proclaim the Message of Jesus

God did not just command us to be a witness, but He also commissioned us to be one. God, in His desire to see mankind delivered from sin, has commissioned those who believe on Him to go forth and carry His message of hope to the world.

Given the Ministry and the Message

Read 2 Corinthians 5:18-20. Who is "all this" (the ministry of reconciliation) from?

_____

_____

_____

What is the ministry of reconciliation?

_____

_____

_____

What is the message of reconciliation?

_____

_____

_____

Finish verse 20:

Therefore, we are _____, God making his appeal through us.

Chosen to Bear Fruit

Read John 15:16. Who is the one whom has chosen us?

_____

_____

_____

What have we been appointed to do?

_____

_____

_____

What kind of fruit does Jesus expect us to produce?

_____

_____

_____

C. We Are Given the Power of Jesus

One startling fact about evangelism is that despite all our good intentions, if we do not have the power of God working in our lives, our efforts will be in vain. No person can do the work of God—and that is what evangelism is. All of our efforts will be useless, all our work fruitless, and all our striving in vain if those efforts are not motivated and empowered by the One who has called us. However, once we have received the power of God, we are responsible to do the work of God in evangelizing our community. And, for the record, if we are believers, we have already received the power of God.

The Power of Jesus Given to Believers

Read Acts 1:8. When did Jesus say each believer would receive power?

_____

_____

_____

What is the power for?

_____

_____

_____

Read Ephesians 1:13. When does the Holy Spirit come to a person?

_____

_____

_____

The Authority of Jesus with Each Believer

Read Matthew 28:18-20. Who has all authority?

_____

_____

_____

According to verse 19, what are we to do because of this?

_____

_____

_____

At the end of verse 20, what is the promise given to those who make disciples?

_____

_____

_____

If Jesus is with us, is there any reason that we cannot do what He commands? Why or why not?

_____

_____

_____

Are you willing to walk in Christ's authority and make disciples of the people in your life? Why or why not?

_____

_____

_____

DAY THREE: HOW TO SHARE YOUR FAITH

Although every Christian has been born again through the same shed blood of Jesus and faith in His atoning sacrifice for sin, not every person has taken the same road to get to that common point. Each person's life is different, so each person's testimony is different. There are, however, some common elements in sharing our testimony that we must remember in order to be effective. Later this week, we will walk through a process of writing our personal story, but today we are going to look at some elements of presentation that must accompany sharing our faith with others.

A. Be Passionate

One of the greatest hindrances to effective evangelism is a lack of enthusiasm or passion for the things that Christ has done in our lives. When Christians don't show concern about Jesus and what He has done, unbelievers will suspect that there is not much for them to be concerned about. Christians who parade a joyless, emotionless, static life have forgotten that great encounter they had when they first believed. If we don't have passion for Jesus, we shouldn't attempt to share our faith until we find it again.

The Passion of Jeremiah

Read Jeremiah 20:9. What did Jeremiah say would happen to him if he chose to withhold the Word of the Lord?

_____

_____

_____

Could Jeremiah ever keep from speaking out concerning God? Why or why not?

_____

_____

_____

What is the Word of God like in your heart? Does it burn like fire, or has it fizzled?

_____

_____

_____

The Passion of Paul

Read 1 Corinthians 9:16. How did Paul view his call to preach the gospel?

_____

_____

_____

The term "woe" means "destruction." In light of this, what do you think Paul meant when he said, "Woe to me if I do not preach the gospel"?

_____

_____

_____

The Passion of One Touched by Jesus

Read Luke 8:38-39. What command did Jesus give to this man whom He had set free?

_____

_____

_____

What was the man's response?

_____

_____

_____

How much has Jesus done for you? Who have you told?

_____

_____

_____

B. Be Personal

The only story that we can truly tell with accuracy and conviction is our own. Although, like every other believer, we had to come to faith in Jesus, the path we took to come to that place is unique unto ourselves. In the work of evangelism, the greatest testimony that we can give is one about how Jesus has changed us.

The Testimony of the Apostles

Read Acts 4:20. To what did the apostles testify?

_____

_____

_____

The Command of Jesus

Read John 15:27. What command did Jesus give His disciples?

_____

_____

_____

For what reason did they need to testify?

_____

_____

_____

How long have you been with Jesus? Does this command apply to you as well? Why or why not?

_____

_____

_____

The Example from the Psalmist

Read Psalm 66:16. What did the psalmist tell about?

_____

_____

_____

C. **Be Prepared**

In order for us to effectively share our testimony with others, we have to be prepared ahead of time. I have heard countless testimonies in which an unbeliever would ask a question and the one witnessing would have just the right answer—two days later! It is very important for us to be prepared to share the story we have concerning our relationship to Jesus.

The Command to Be Prepared

Read 1 Peter 3:15. How should we set apart Christ in our heart?

_____

_____

_____

What does it mean to set apart Christ as Lord?

_____

_____

_____

To whom should we be prepared to give an answer?

_____

_____

_____

How often should we be prepared?

_____

_____

_____

What is the reason for the hope that we have been given?

_____

_____

_____

What two criteria are given in this passage for sharing of our testimony?

1. _____

2. _____

Prepared to Speak Out

Read 2 Timothy 4:1-2. What charge did Paul give to Timothy in this passage?

_____

_____

_____

When should a person be prepared to preach the Word?

_____

_____

_____

What three distinctive elements of preaching the Word are included here?

1. _____

2. _____

3. _____

How should the preaching of the Word be done?

    1. With complete _____

    2. And _____ .

DAY FOUR: YOU HAVE A TESTIMONY

As mentioned previously, in sharing what we believe and what we have come to know to be true, we need to understand that we have a testimony that is specifi c and unique. The world is looking for the truth of what we say in the lives that we live; that is to say, our actions must accompany our words. These two elements define the parameters of our personal testimony—our actions and our words. If the Lord Jesus Christ has changed our lives, the world is looking to see it and is listening to hear about it. We need to know what to share.

Today we are going to see that the nature of our testimony is more than just how we came to know Jesus; it is also how we are now living with Jesus. Before we can share our testimony, we need to understand what it is and its importance in the lives of those around us.

A. Our Testimony Is Seen in How We Live

It has been said that the way in which we live our lives puts the punctuation on the words that we say. That which we do will either bring into question or will give exclamation to our testimony. The only true and valid testimony is found in the lives of God's people who are actively living out the Word of God.

Seen in a Courageous Life

Read Acts 4:13. What was seen in the lives of Peter and John?

_____

_____

_____

What was the reaction of the Sanhedrin?

_____

_____

_____

What did the Sanhedrin recognize in Peter and John?

_____

_____

_____

Testimony Invalidated by Actions

Read Titus 1:16. Who did "they" profess to know?

_____

_____

_____

By their works, what did "they" do?

_____

_____

_____

What three descriptions are given to these people?

1. _____

2. _____

3. _____

B. Our Testimony Is Heard in What We Say

No one ever escaped drowning by watching someone else swim. In the same way, no one ever escaped judgment by watching someone else live. If we are going to reach others with the message of hope—a message that we have heard and believed—then we need to share it with others. Until we are willing to open our mouths and speak, many people will end up without the hope of eternal life.

A Testimony Found in the Heart

Read Matthew 12:34. From where did Jesus say the words of our mouth originate?

_____

_____

_____

Read 1 John 5:10. How does a person acquire the necessary testimony?

_____

_____

_____

What has the person done who chooses not to believe God?

_____

_____

_____

A Testimony of Hope

Read 1 John 5:11-12. This text begins, "And this is the testimony." Write out in the space provided what that testimony is.

_____

_____

_____

A Testimony to Be Spoken

Read 1 Corinthians 2:1-5. What was it that Paul proclaimed?

_____

_____

_____

In verse 2, what did he decide to know?

_____

_____

_____

How did Paul present his message and preaching?

_____

_____

_____

What was the purpose of this (verse 5)?

_____

_____

_____

DAY FIVE: WRITING OUT YOUR STORY

One of the hardest tasks of developing our own personal testimony is how to present it to others. All of us know what has taken place in our own lives, but developing that knowledge into a workable presentation for others to understand takes some work.

Today's work may seem a bit simple at first, but when you get involved in it, you will find that it does take some effort. Today, you will be writing your story. You will be incorporating four elements in your story: (1) the time before you knew Christ, (2) the story of how you met Christ, (3) the truth of having Christ in your life, and (4) your testimony of needing Christ. Each of these elements will be explained in greater detail below. We will take this outline directly from the testimony of the apostle Paul as he shared it with King Agrippa in Acts 26.

A. The Time Before You Knew Christ (Acts 26:1-11)

This is the starting point for all testimonies. You need to be able to recall with those whom you are sharing what your life was like without Jesus. So, what was your life like before you came to know the salvation of Jesus? Write it in the space below.

_____

_____

_____

B. The Story of How You Met Christ (Acts 26:12-18)

This is the part in which you explain what events took place that made you realize you needed Jesus to save you. Who shared with you? When did you understand? How did you ask Christ to come in to your life? Write your encounter with Jesus in the space below.

_____

_____

_____

C. The Truth of Having Jesus in Your Life (Acts 26:19-24)

This is the part in which you explain what Jesus has done for you. What is your life like now? What have you seen changed in your life? What has He called you to? How are you living to please Him today? Write briefly about your life with Jesus in the space below.

_____

_____

_____

D. Your Testimony of Needing Christ (Acts 26:25-32)

This is the part in which you explain that all people—even the people with whom you are sharing—need to know the saving grace of Jesus. Your testimony will be lacking if you do not bring the person to the understanding that he or she needs Jesus. Write what you would say to another person about his or her need for Jesus.

_____

_____

_____

DAY SIX: TIME FOR REVIEW

Below are five review sections, one for each day. Try to do them without referring back to the lesson. Recheck your work and bring any questions you have to class.

Day One

What are the four essentials for evangelism?

1. _____

2. _____

3. _____

4. _____

Day Two

What are the three reasons we are called to share Jesus?

1. _____

2. _____

3. _____

Day Three

What three elements are involved in how we share our faith?

1. Be _____

2. Be _____

3. Be _____

Day Four

What are the two natures of a personal testimony?

1. _____

2. _____

Day Five

Write out your personal testimony on a separate sheet of paper to share with the class.

Memory Verse

Write out your Scripture verse for the week from memory:

_____

_____

_____

CHAPTER 8

WHAT IS YET TO COME

> **Memory Verse:** *"He who testifi es to these things says, 'Surely, I am coming soon.' Amen. Come, Lord Jesus!"*
>
> (Revelation 22:20)

SOME OF THE greatest debates and contentions in the Christian church center on people's understanding of what is yet to come. The study of the end times and the final events of history is called *eschatology*. The word "eschatology" comes from the Greek word *eschatos*, which means "last." Simply put, eschatology is the study of last things.

Although Scripture gives us some clues and markers of what is yet to come, it does not fill in all the details of God's activity that will happen in the future. This week's lesson is not to try to figure out the future through some prophetic exercise, but to try to gain an understanding of what God has revealed to us concerning what is yet to come.

Questions that inevitably come up in conversations concerning this topic are: Are we in the last days? When will Jesus return? How long until the end? What will be the sign? What is the tribulation? What is heaven like? A host of other questions, as numerous as the inquisitors, are heard time and time again. This week, we will try to unlock some of the mysteries surrounding what is yet to come.

DAY ONE: THE "LAST DAYS" ARE UPON US

To answer the question of whether or not we are in the last days, the answer is YES! We are in the last days; that is to say, we are in the final period of God's redemptive plan for mankind. However, we must understand that God doesn't keep a timetable as we do in His plan for the redemption of the world. As Peter states in 2 Peter 3:8-9:

But do not overlook this one fact, beloved, that with the Lord one day is as a thousand years, and a thousand years as one day. The Lord is not slow to fulfill his promise as some count slowness, but is patient toward you, not wishing that any should perish, but that all should reach repentance.

Do not look on the idea of being in the last days as necessarily a length of time but as a period in God's redemptive plan. No one knows how long the last days will last. We only know that we are in the midst of them.

A. The Beginning of the End

One striking question is when the last days actually began. There are several opinions concerning this. Some have said that the last days began when John the Baptist came on the scene. Others say that it was when Jesus was born. Still others say that it began at the time of the crucifixion or the resurrection. In fact, Scripture makes it clear when the last days of God's redemptive plan began.

When the Spirit Came upon the Church

Read Acts 2:17-18. Fill in the missing words from verse 17:

And in the _____, God declares, _____

my _____ on all flesh.

According to verse 18, who will receive the Spirit of the Lord?

_____

_____

_____

According to the Prophetic Message of Joel

Read Joel 2:28-32. The beginning of this text says: "afterward." This can also mean "in the course of time," indicating something done at the appropriate time. What is done afterward?

_____

_____

_____

What will happen at the end of the last days (verse 31)?

_____

_____

_____

B. The Evidence of the Last Days

Jesus chastised the Pharisees and Sadducees for their failure to understand the times in which they were living. In Matthew 16:1-3, Jesus exclaimed that they could interpret the signs of the weather but could not understand the signs of the times. The Bible gives us ample information to understand the times in which we now live.

Terrible Times in the Last Days

Read 2 Timothy 3:1-5. What does Paul state in verse 1?

_____

_____

_____

In verses 2 to 5, Paul lists 18 indicators of the last days. List each of these below.

1. _____ 2. _____ 3. _____

4. _____ 5. _____ 6. _____

7. _____ 8. _____ 9. _____

10. _____ 11. _____ 12. _____

13. _____ 14. _____ 15. _____

16. _____ 17. _____ 18. _____

What appearance will these indicators take? What will they deny?

_____

_____

_____

What command is given at the end of verse 5?

_____

_____

_____

Do you see evidence of these indicators in the time you are living in now? If so, what indicators have you observed?

_____

_____

_____

A Falling Away from the Church

Read 1 John 2:18-19. What does John say about the times in which we live?

_____

_____

_____

Who is to come in the last hour?

_____

_____

_____

What does John say at the end of verse 18?

_____

_____

_____

In verse 19, we are given some indicators of how we are to know it is the last hour. What evidence is given?

_____

_____

_____

Have you seen a marked falling away from those who claim to know Jesus?

_____

_____

_____

C. How to Endure in These Trying Times

Knowing that we are in the last days is of little help if it doesn't inspire us to live at a higher level in our Christian lives. We have been given some guidelines to follow concerning what it takes to endure in the final hour of the redemptive plan of God. We have already read some troubling information concerning the times in which we live. Now we need to know how to endure.

Be Prepared to Pray

Read 1 Peter 4:7. According to this text, what is near?

_____

_____

_____

What two things must we do because the end of all things is near?

1. _____

2. _____

What is the purpose of our being sober minded and self-controlled?

_____

_____

_____

What does it mean to be sober minded?

_____

_____

_____

What does it mean to be self-controlled?

_____

_____

_____

First Peter 4: 8-11 captures for us the picture of Christian living. List below those things from the text that you need to do or do better.

_____

_____

_____

DAY TWO: JESUS IS COMING SOON

The great hope of every Christian is the return of our Lord and Savior, Jesus Christ. We live looking forward to that day, hoping that His return will be soon. Many people have tried to determine the specifi c time that Jesus will return to the earth. Several have even stated a specific day or time that Jesus would come again. However, it is not for us to try and determine when Jesus will return but to be ready whenever He appears.

For our study today, we are going to remain in one text: Matthew 24:3-44. In this passage, the disciples came to Jesus privately and asked Him the very question that we have been discussing: When would He return. The disciples asked in verse three: "Tell us, when will these things be, and what will be the sign of your coming and of the end of the age?" In the remaining verses, Jesus speaks to this very issue.

A. Signs of His Return

Many, if not all, Christians have asked the same question the apostles asked at one time or another in their lives. If we are true to our faith, we are looking forward to that day when our Savior will return. Jesus gives us some clear signs of His soon-coming return.

The Appearance of False Christs

Read Matthew 24:4-5. What command does Jesus give us in verse 4?

_____

_____

_____

What reason does Jesus give in verse 5 as to why we are to be watchful?

_____

_____

_____

Have you ever heard of anyone claiming to be the Christ? If so, what was the situation?

_____

_____

_____

What will be the result of these false Christs coming?

_____

_____

_____

Other Signs of the Coming of Jesus

Read Matthew 24:6-8,14. What are the five signs given in these verses for the coming of Jesus?

1. _____

2. _____

3. _____

4. _____

5. _____

What does verse 8 say concerning these various signs?

_____

_____

_____

Have you heard of any of these signs taking place in our world today? If so, list some below.

_____

_____

_____

B. Times and Dates

As previously mentioned, many have tried, unsuccessfully, to predict the time and day that Jesus will return. In fact, a variety of religions have built doctrine around their predicted day of the return of the Lord and even published books concerning their prognostications. However, Scripture is clear about who will and will not know when that day will arrive.

Only the Father Knows

Read Matthew 24:36. Finish the verse: "But concerning that day and hour...

no one _____ not even _____ nor _____, but

the _____ only."

Why do you think the Son is kept from knowing this?

_____

_____

The Actions that We Are to Take

Read Matthew 24:42. What actions are we to take as we wait for the day of the Lord's return?

_____

_____

_____

What does it mean to keep watch? (See also Matthew 26:41; 1 Corinthians 16:13; Colossians 4:2; 1 Peter 5:8; Revelation 16:15)

_____

_____

_____

What is the reason we are to keep watch?

_____

_____

_____

The Warning to Be Ready

Read Matthew 24:44. What is the warning that Jesus gives?

_____

_____

_____

What is the hour that Jesus will come?

_____

_____

_____

C. Our Final and Only Hope

The issue of the Christian faith is the continual hope in complete redemption through Jesus. That redemption is made complete when Jesus is revealed and returns to claim those who are His own. Redemption for us as believers begins at conversion, is carried through life as we are transformed by faith through the sanctification of the Spirit, and is culminated in the final redemption of our bodies at the resurrection. The final hope that we have is seen in the coming of Jesus when He will call His own to meet Him in the air.

Hanging on for the Long Haul

Read Matthew 24:9-13. According to verse 9, what situation may followers of Jesus face?

_____

_____

_____

What will many do because of this persecution (verse 10)?

_____

_____

_____

Who will appear when many turn away from the faith? What will they do (verse 11)?

_____

_____

_____

According to verse 12, what will increase? What will happen because of this?

_____

_____

_____

In verse 13, what requirement does Jesus state is necessary for salvation?

_____

_____

_____

Why do you think it is necessary to stand firm to the end?

_____

_____

_____

DAY THREE: UNDERSTANDING THE "GREAT TRIBULATION"

To explain the Great Tribulation in detail is nearly impossible given the small amount of time we have in today's study. A multitude of books have been written on the subject. Movies and dramatic performances have inundated the theatres. What we will discuss today is an overview of the final judgment of God and how it plays out in the machinations of God's redemptive plan.

There is only one passage of Scripture that actually designates this period in God's redemptive plan as the Great Tribulation. In Revelation 7:14 we read, "I answered, 'Sir, you know.' And he said, 'These are they who have come out of the great tribulation.'" The term "tribulation" simply means affliction. Thus, this time of tribulation is a time of great and terrible affliction that comes upon the entire world.

A. God's Final Judgment

Regardless of when the last days actually began, the last period of the last days is considered to be the time of God's final judgment. This period of God's redemptive plan is described in Revelation chapters 6–19. In these chapters, we see in great detail what takes place during the time of this affliction. For our study, we will not go into this in detail but will focus on two things: God's promise of final judgment and God's purpose for final judgment.

God's Promise of Final Judgment

Read 2 Peter 3:6-7,10-12. How did God judge the world the first time, and by what method did God bring destruction?

_____

_____

For what are the present heavens and earth being stored up?

_____

_____

_____

For what are they being kept?

_____

_____

_____

According to verse 10, what will happen to God's creation on the day of judgment?

    1. The heavens: _____

    2. The heavenly bodies: _____

    3. The earth: _____

What kind of lives should Christians live because they know about this coming judgment?

_____

_____

_____

God's Purpose for Final Judgment

The Revealing of His Son

Read Matthew 25:31. How will the Son of Man come?

_____

_____

_____

Who will be coming with Him?

_____

_____

_____

Where will He be seated?

_____

_____

_____

The Separation of the Nations

Read Matthew 25:32-33. Who will be gathered before Him?

_____

_____

_____

What will be the purpose for the gathering?

_____

_____

_____

The Dispensation of Judgment

Read Matthew 25:46. Where will the wicked go?

_____

_____

_____

Where will the righteous go?

_____

_____

_____

B. The "Fairness" of God

Many people have argued that God is unfair in punishing people. After all, if God is love, why would He send people to an eternal fire or cast them away from His presence? Those who speak like this are making a human argument for the human condition and have no reference to the nature of God. We need to understand the judgment of God from God's perspective and not our own. If we examine the nature and character of God, we will see the reality of our sinfulness and the measures that God has taken to provide us a way of escape from the corruption of the world.

The Nature and Character of God

Read Isaiah 6:3-5. What description of God were the seraphs calling out?

_____

_____

_____

Note that the seraphs used the word "holy" three times. Why do you think this is significant?

_____

_____

_____

What is the whole earth full of concerning God (see also Psalm 19:1)?

_____

_____

_____

In verse 5, what was Isaiah's reaction?

_____

_____

_____

Why did he react this way?

_____

_____

_____

Sin Must Be Punished

Read Romans 2:1-16. According to verse 2, how does God's judgment fall and on whom?

_____

_____

_____

According to verse 5, for what two reasons do people store up wrath for the day of God's wrath?

1. _____

2. _____

According to verse 12, who is it that will be subject to judgment?

_____

_____

_____

In verse 16, what will God judge? Is there anything that can be hidden from God?

_____

_____

The Way of Escape Received or Rejected

Read John 3:18. What is the requirement to avoid the condemnation of God?

_____

_____

_____

If a person does not believe, how does he or she stand before God?

_____

_____

_____

Can a person avoid the judgment of God without Jesus? Why or why not?

_____

_____

_____

Do you know anyone who doesn't know Jesus? Is that person condemned already? What will you do?

_____

_____

_____

C. Will Christians Have to Endure This?

Many books, lectures and papers have been spoken, read and written concerning the Christian's role in the final judgment of God. Today, there are three primary views on whether or not Christians will have to go through the Great Tribulation. Each of these positions defines the catching away or "rapture" of the church based upon the period of time that they believe it will take place: before the tribulation (pre-tribulation), during the tribulation (mid-tribulation), or after the tribulation (post-tribulation). What does the Bible teach concerning this event?

The Plan for God's People

Read 1 Thessalonians 5:9-10. Fill in the missing words from verse 9:

For God has not _____ us for _____

but to obtain _____ through our Lord Jesus Christ.

In verse 10, what is one of the benefits that believers receive from the sacrifice of Jesus?

_____

_____

_____

Have Christians been appointed to suffer the wrath of God? Why or why not?

_____

_____

_____

The Period of God's "Rapture"

Read 1 Thessalonians 4:16-18. Who is it that comes down from heaven?

_____

_____

_____

What will accompany Him? What will be the result of His command?

_____

_____

_____

What will those of us experience who remain alive and belong to Jesus?

_____

_____

_____

How long will we be with the Lord?

_____

_____

_____

What should we do with this information (verse 18)?

_____

_____

_____

(A thought to consider: in the book of Revelation, after chapter 3 and until chapter 19, the church is not found on the earth.)

Day Four: After We Die

Many people view death as the great "undiscovered country." They have never been there, so death is a great mystery to them—an unknown journey that they are scared to take but know that they must eventually travel. This is perhaps one of the greatest fears of mankind—that death is unavoidable. However, unknown to most people, we can have a glimpse into the reality of death and the journey that people go on when they die. Death does not have to be a mystery, and is not to those who are willing to investigate. Today, we are going to try and investigate the nature and reality of death.

A. So I've Died. Now What?

Death is a one-per-person reality. While there are only two people in all of history who have avoided death—Enoch and Elijah—and very few who have ever come back from death, there is only one who has ever truly conquered death: our Lord Jesus. Thus, for us to understand what death is about and what is to come after it, we need to go to the one who truly conquered death and now has power over it. In Scripture, there are a variety of texts that discuss the nature and reality of death. Today, we are going to look at two aspects of death found in these passages: the death of the righteous and the death of the wicked.

The Death of the Righteous

Read Philippians 1:21. What is the primary reason for a Christian to live?

_____

_____

_____

For you, what does "to live is Christ" mean?

_____

_____

_____

What is it considered when a Christian dies?

_____

_____

_____

Why do you think the apostle Paul called it gain to die?

_____

_____

_____

Do you consider it gain to die? Why or why not?

_____

_____

_____

The Death of the Wicked

Read Revelation 21:8. What are the eight categories of the wicked listed in this text?

1. _____   5. _____

2. _____   6. _____

3. _____   7. _____

4. _____   8. _____

What will be the final place for those described in this text?

_____

_____

_____

What is the one key element that each of these categories share?

_____

_____

_____

B. Concerning the Death of Children

Many Christians are deeply concerned about what happens when children die. The primary concern involves the nature of their salvation and whether or not they are to be held accountable for their sins in the presence of God. The Jews held the tradition that a child was not accountable to the Law of God until he or she reached the age of *Bar Mitzvah*, which means "Son of the Commandments." At this age, traditionally 13, the child would be held accountable as an adult for his or her responsibility to the Law. However, this is simply a tradition and not necessarily biblical. So the question remains: what does the Bible say concerning the death of children? Because Scripture does not deal with the death of children directly, we must take our cue from the character of God.

The Call of Jesus

Read Matthew 19:13-14. What was the disciples' reaction when the children were brought to Jesus?

_____

_____

_____

What was Jesus' command regarding the children?

_____

_____

_____

To whom did Jesus say the kingdom of heaven belongs?

_____

_____

_____

Why do you think Jesus used children as an example of those who belong to His kingdom?

_____

_____

_____

A Biblical Example

Read 2 Samuel 12:15-23. For what was David fasting and praying?

_____

_____

_____

When the child died, what did David tell his servants concerning the infant's death?

_____

_____

_____

What do you think David meant when he said, "I shall go to him, but he will not return to me?"

_____

_____

_____

C. What About the Resurrection?

The resurrection of Jesus and the hope of resurrection that every believer has is the central theme of the gospel narrative. The fact is, if there is no resurrection then there is no salvation; and if there is no salvation then we are all doomed to an eternity apart from God. However, Jesus Christ was raised from the dead, and He promised His servants that they would also be raised to a new life.

The Promise of Resurrection

Read John 11:25-26. According to this passage, is the resurrection an event or a person?

_____

_____

_____

If the resurrection is a person, what is needed for someone to participate in it?

_____

_____

_____

Do you believe in the promise of the resurrection? Why or why not?

_____

_____

_____

The Power of Resurrection

Read 1 Peter 1:3-5. What has a believer received from the resurrection of Jesus as described in verse 3?

_____

_____

_____

What is the nature of the inheritance that believers receive as described in verse 4?

_____

_____

_____

How is the believer shielded until the coming of the salvation of God?

_____

_____

_____

The Future Fulfillment of Resurrection

Read Revelation 20:6. What two words describe those who have part in the first resurrection?

1. _____

2. _____

What will have no power over those who take part in the first resurrection?

_____

_____

_____

What is the second death (see Revelation 21:8)?

_____

_____

_____

DAY FIVE: A GLIMPSE OF HEAVEN

One of the most common questions that people ask is what heaven is going to be like. The simple fact is that the mortal human mind cannot hope to comprehend the incredible glory of heaven that will be revealed to those who believe. The apostle Paul stated this in Romans 8:18: "For I consider that the sufferings of this present time are not worth comparing with the glory that is to be revealed to us." Yet if we insist on wanting to know what heaven will be like, then it is only reasonable to ask the one who came from there and then returned.

God wants us to have a glimpse of glory. It is the steadfast hope in all of us that there will be a day when we will depart this world and enter into the final and ultimate rest that has been promised to every believer in Christ Jesus. Remember the words of the apostle Paul in 1 Corinthians 13:12: "For now we see in a mirror dimly, but then face to face. Now I know in part; then I shall know fully, even as I have been fully known."

A. The Revealing of Eternity

God desires for those who belong to Him to have an awareness, even though it might be dim, of what eternity will be like. The book of Revelation describes in detail the glimpse of glory that we will see. This book is the unveiling of the future home for the saints of God.

The New Jerusalem

Read Revelation 21:9-14. In verse 11, how did the new city shine?

_____

_____

What are the 12 gates?

_____

_____

_____

What are the 12 foundations?

_____

_____

_____

The Light of the Glory of Heaven

Read Revelation 21:22-27. What is meant by this: "Its temple is the Lord God Almighty and the Lamb" (verse 22)?

_____

_____

_____

Who gives light to the city?

_____

_____

_____

Who is allowed to enter into the city?

_____

_____

_____

B. The Dwelling of God

Of all the things we can learn about heaven, the most dominant theme is that it is the place where God dwells. The final reward of our lives is to be in the very presence of almighty God and to dwell in His house forever!

Read Revelation 21:3-5. Where will the dwelling of God be?

_____

_____

_____

What is the promise concerning the presence of God?

_____

_____

_____

What four things will be no more in the presence of God?

1. _____

2. _____

3. _____

4. _____

How is God making everything?

_____

_____

_____

C. In the Presence of God

Read Revelation 22:3-5. According to verse 3, what will be gone?

_____

_____

_____

What will believers finally be able to see?

_____

_____

_____

Why will God's name be on the believers' foreheads?

_____

_____

_____

How long will they reign with Him?

_____

_____

_____

D. The Promise for Every Person

The promise of eternal life and the glory of God are for every person who believes. God wants everyone to come to Him by faith and trust in the complete work of Jesus for salvation. Even at the end of the book of Revelation, there is the call for any who are willing to come and receive. The promise is for all people, provided they come by faith.

The Father's Call

Read Revelation 21:6. What is the requirement for someone to come and receive?

_____

_____

_____

What is the promise to those who come that are thirsty?

_____

_____

_____

The Son's Warning

Read Revelation 22:12. What is the warning that Jesus gives?

_____

_____

_____

What is He bringing with Him?

_____

_____

_____

How will Jesus divide the rewards?

_____

_____

_____

The Call of the Spirit and of the Church

Read Revelation 22:17. What do the Spirit, the bride and whoever hears call people to do?

_____

_____

_____

To what are they to come?

_____

_____

_____

What are the two requirements that are given for those who come?

    1. Whoever is _____

    2. Whoever _____

What is the cost to receive the water of life?

_____

_____

_____

DAY SIX: TIME FOR REVIEW

Below are five review sections, one for each day. Try and do them without referring back to the lesson. Recheck your work and bring any questions you have to class.

Day One

Write out 5 of the 18 indicators of the last days given in 2 Timothy 3:1-5.

    1. _____   4. _____

    2. _____   5. _____

    3. _____

Day Two

List two of the five signs of Jesus' return given in Matthew 24.

1. _____

2. _____

Day Three

According to 2 Peter 3, what two means does God use to judge the whole earth?

1. _____

2. _____

Day Four

What did Jesus say in John 11:25-26 concerning the resurrection?

_____

_____

_____

Day Five

In the city of the New Jerusalem, what are the 12 gates?

_____

_____

_____

What are the 12 foundations?

_____

_____

_____

For extra credit, what were their names?

	Tribes of Israel	Apostles
1.		
2.		
3.		
4.		
5.		
6.		
7.		
8.		
9.		
10.		
11.		
12.		

Memory Verse

Write out your Scripture verse for the week from memory:

_____

_____

_____

THE END

CONGRATULATIONS! YOU'VE WORKED your way through a study that is the start of a long journey of faithfully walking with Christ. I strongly encourage you to seek out your pastor and ask that person to help guide you to greater levels of Christian growth and opportunities for service. Gather with God's people as often as possible and get involved as deeply as you can. Our Lord Jesus said, "Well done, good and faithful servant. You have been faithful over a little; I will set you over much. Enter into the joy of your master." (Matthew 25:21). Always remember that your faithfulness is God's delight.

In Christ's service,
Rev. Michael Duncan

For more information about
Michael Duncan
or to purchase his other books
please visit:
www.authormichaelduncan.com

Invite Michael to speak at your event
by contacting him at his website.

or visit him at his church:
www.faithcommunitychurchos.org

Made in the USA
Las Vegas, NV
02 February 2023

66738723R00109